FOR YOUR
CONSIDERATION

Keanu
Reeves

For our loved ones, good ones, and The One

Library of Congress Cataloging in Publication Number: 2019936801

ISBN: 978-1-68369-151-8

Printed in the United States of America

Typeset in Century, Adobe Caslon Pro, and Avenir

Text by Larissa Zageris and Kitty Curran
Designed by Aurora Parlagreco
Cover illustration by Mercedes deBellard
Interior illustrations by Ben Mounsey-Wood
Production management by John J. McGurk

Quirk Books
215 Church Street
Philadelphia, PA 19106
quirkbooks.com

10 9 8 7 6 5 4 3 2 1

FOR YOUR
CONSIDERATION

Keanu
Reeves

Larissa Zageris and
Kitty Curran

QUIRK BOOKS

PHILADELPHIA

Table of Contents

A Brief History of
Keanu Reeves

September 2, 1964: Keanu is born a Virgo

1979: Keanu plays Mercutio in a production of
Romeo & Juliet

1981: Keanu drops out of high school to do theater

1984: Keanu moves to Los Angeles to try his hand at
Hollywood

January 31, 1986: *Young Blood*

May 8, 1986: *River's Edge*

December 19, 1986: *Babes in Toyland*

1988: Keanu is in a serious motorcycle accident and has his
spleen removed

April 22, 1988: *Permanent Record*

December 11, 1988: *Dangerous Liaisons*

February 17, 1989: *Bill & Ted's Excellent Adventure*

December 17, 1989: *The Tracey Ullman Show*

1990: *Bill & Ted's Excellent Adventures* (animated series)

1991: Dogstar, the "folk-thrash" band is formed, with Keanu on bass

July 12, 1991: *Point Break*

July 19, 1991: *Bill & Ted's Bogus Journey*

July 20, 1991: *My Own Private Idaho*

November 13, 1992: *Bram Stoker's Dracula*

July 2, 1993: *Much Ado About Nothing*

May 25, 1994: *Little Buddha*

June 10, 1994: *Speed*

1995: Keanu refuses role in *Speed 2: Cruise Control*; stars in Manitoba Theatre Center's production of *Hamlet*

May 26, 1995: *Johnny Mnemonic*

August 11, 1995: *A Walk in the Clouds*

August 2, 1996: *Chain Reaction*

September 13, 1996: *Feeling Minnesota*

October 17, 1997: *The Devil's Advocate*

March 31, 1999: *The Matrix*

August 11, 2000: *The Replacements*

September 8, 2000: *The Watcher*

January 19, 2001: *The Gift*

February 16, 2001: *Sweet November*

September 14, 2001: *Hardball*

May 15, 2003: *The Matrix Reloaded*

June 3, 2003: *The Animatrix*

November 5, 2003: *The Matrix Revolutions*

December 12, 2003: *Something's Gotta Give*

2004: Keanu receives a star on the Hollywood Walk of Fame

February 18, 2005: *Constantine*

June 16, 2006: *The Lake House*

July 28, 2006: *A Scanner Darkly*

April 11, 2008: *Street Kings*

December 12, 2008: *The Day the Earth Stood Still*

July 10, 2009: *The Private Lives of Pippa Lee*

May 2010: First appearance of Sad Keanu meme

June 15, 2010: Fans create "Cheer Up Keanu" Day in response to the Sad Keanu meme

2011: Keanu cofounds Arch Motorcycle Company with Gard Hollinger

January 14, 2011: Keanu produces his first film, *Henry's Crime*

April 21, 2011: Keanu publishes *Ode to Happiness*, a grown-up picture book

August 17, 2012: Keanu co-produces *Side by Side*, a documentary about digital and photographic film

May 28, 2013: *Generation Um . . .*

July 5, 2013: Keanu makes his directorial debut with his Tiger Chen collaboration, *Man of Tai Chi*

December 25, 2013: *47 Ronin*

October 24, 2014: *John Wick*

October 9, 2015: *Knock Knock*

2016: *Swedish Dicks* (TV series)

April 29, 2016: *Keanu*

June 24, 2016: *The Neon Demon*

February 10, 2017: *John Wick: Chapter 2*

June 23, 2017: *The Bad Batch*

July 13, 2018: *Siberia*

August 2, 2018: *Destination Wedding*

September 21, 2018: *A Happening of Monumental Proportions*

January 11, 2019: *Replicas*

May 17, 2019: *John Wick: Chapter 3 – Parabellum*

May 29, 2019: *Always Be My Maybe*

June 21, 2019: *Toy Story 4*

Introduction

We grew up taking Keanu Reeves for granted, first as the sweet but dimwitted kid in *Bill and Ted's Excellent Adventure*, then as a complicated heartthrob in *Point Break* and *My Own Private Idaho*, and later as a full-bore action hero in *Speed* and *The Matrix*. Between the blockbusters, we embraced him ironically as he was cast (and miscast) in a dizzying array of prestige and genre movies that we rented from our local video store on Friday nights.

For a certain generation of fans—that nebulous space between Gen X and Millennial—Keanu was both an object of desire and an afterthought. But the irony of loving someone ironically is how earnest that devotion can become. And in our moment in culture, it's not hard to earnestly appreciate the man who has launched a thousand internet memes—and inspired the era in which we currently live: the Keanussance.

But why the need for irony in the first place? Much of the reason is Keanu's style of acting.

Often charged with being "blank" or "expressionless," he is blank much as a piece of paper is. He gets filled up by his role, the story, our perceptions, and the ideas he invites us to form with a look through his long-ass bangs or a gesture you could blink and miss. He is a cipher, but he's also active and present, inviting the audience into worlds built for their entertainment, not just for his celebrity.

And Keanu is, admittedly, not a knowable celebrity. He rejects the traditional trappings of stardom in favor of walking the path of the artist, often in a perfect-fitting T-shirt and well-worn suede boots. He likes his privacy. He selects movies based on his own secret criteria, an algorithm which meant that we saw him in *A Scanner Darkly* and *The Lake House* back-to-back in 2006. (This was the beginning of what would be a notable commercial dip in his career, before he reascended with *John Wick*.) He is enigmatic but clearly driven by his own desires and interests. We can't pin him down, and that's part of the fun.

At the same time, he's made a career of learning new things his Thing, all while steering clear of the outsize and awful behavior typically expected (though definitely not encouraged) of a male star. His vulnerability, his love of art and literature, and his long-running friendships with female co-stars like Sandra Bullock and Winona Ryder make him a tender and complicated example of nontoxic masculinity—or, at the very least, a person striving to be kind and excellent in work and in life. In this endeavor, he helps us imagine that we could be ourselves but better, too.

In this book, we will explore what we talk about when we talk about Keanu because we believe he merits study. We will riff lovingly on his persona between critical essays because we're your cool teachers who let you pass notes and eat candy in class. We've never met him personally, but we've grown up with him, in a sense. To us he seems decent. He seems good. He seems actively engaged. In the words of the man himself: "The simple act of paying attention can take you a long way."

Let's pay Keanu Reeves some attention.

PART I

Keanussance Man

A beautiful man takes shape at the base of a loading dock. He wears blood like a fine suit. He wears a fine suit beneath the blood. His brutal form is wrung and well-written: the lines of his face cut light and kiss shadow; the bow of his broad shoulders braces for the inevitable; his eyes flicker with pain. He's had the shit kicked out of him. He looks like he's kicked the shit out of them, too—whoever they are. You get the gut-punch sense that the pain this man carries cuts deeper than run-of-the mill, state-of-the-art, blunt-force trauma. This guy, your guy, our guy: he dances every night in the bad-man ballet, but tonight's performance will be his last.

He's got a broken heart.

But the show must go on.

The man slumps against the dock. He looks at his blood-spattered phone. He takes a ragged, measured breath—then allows the rest of the movie to begin.

Introducing Keanu Reeves as "The Baba Yaga"

Anyone who has seen *John Wick* instantly recognizes this scene. It's a killer way to open a movie about a formerly retired assassin out to avenge his dog while grieving his wife. It also serves as an overture to our Keanu's return to pop cultural prominence.

He is breathtaking in this 2014 sleeper hit, but he has been breathtaking before. He's been deft and daft and scary. He's been a lover, a fighter, and a hopeful time traveler. He's used a magic mailbox to fall for Sandra Bullock and an ocean to fall for Patrick Swayze. He's shared cupcakes with Loneliness, beaten Death, and outwitted the Devil himself—twice. He's been redeemed, he's been creamed, he's been funny, he's been a good listener. He's been intimate and inarticulate, tender and terrifying, wyld and soft. He's been to hell—and he's been a kitten.

He's also created this entire varied, interested, and interesting career that has lasted for thirty years (and counting) while getting bagged on consistently by the press and the public. He has been constantly cursed for his "blankness." His good roles have been chalked up to dumb luck or good looks and thirsty audiences. He's long been damned to be as "dumb" as Ted "Theodore" Logan from the Bill & Ted movies—a role he first played (to acclaim) in 1989.

He has been referred to as someone who uses "surfer speak" with painful frequency by a culture that held only the briefest exploitable interest in surfing. The government won't allow us to tell you just how many unimaginative headlines have been written about Keanu that play on the words "dude" or "whoa," but it's safe to say they outnumber all of the Agent Smiths in *The Matrix Reloaded*.

He has been referred to, more than once, as having the versatility and screen presence of a wooden plank.

But that was then. Now, we live in the heady days of four-*John-Wicks*-and-a-TV-show Keanu; of multiple thoughtful (even worshipful) think pieces about Keanu and his acting abilities (see Alex Pappademas's April 2019 feature in *GQ*, appropriately entitled "The Legend of Keanu Reeves," and Angelica Jade Bastien's "The Grace of Keanu Reeves"); scores of tweets singing the praises of how this one immortal man has singlehandedly and secretly provided the budgets of children's hospitals/reinvented modern action cinema/restored hope for the concept of men in general and served as the literal face of a wellspring of memes and GIFs appropriate for any emotion or occasion.

So . . .

Pop quiz, hot shot.

Why are we *really* in the midst of the Keanussance?

. . . And why now?

In the '80s There Was Keanu, and He Was Good

We can start trying to answer these questions by hopping in our nearest time-traveling phone booth and journeying back to the mid-1980s and the start of Keanu's career. Our best twenty-year-old Toronto boy headed for the hills—the Hollywood Hills!—with hope in his heart and hair in his eyes.

Keanu kicked off his life in pictures with a series of roles that won him acclaim for being a soulful performer with a heck of a range. He played haunted and hangdog to poetic perfection in *River's Edge* and *Permanent Record* and punk-rock romanced Amy Madigan in *The Prince of Pennsylvania*. He also used his wiles on Uma Thurman *and* Glenn Close (!) in *Dangerous Liaisons* before regretfully dueling with a fiendish John Malkovich to the death in this eighteenth-century French tale of sociopathic lovers with nothing better to do than destroy one another with well-timed letters.

Whether rocking an asymmetrical haircut or the inner conflict of the teenager/chevalier he was playing at the moment, baby Keanu brought an engagement to his roles that highlighted his performance and enhanced whatever his co-stars were doing. He never phoned anything in, and the result was a palpable screen presence that didn't over-shadow so much as support the world being made onscreen. We now know that these were the early days of Keanu developing his hallmark subdued-but-vital style of actively listening to his scene partners and sharing space with them. Critics and fans took keen notice of his approach—and his undeniable, androgynous beauty.

Keanu was gorgeous in a way most mallrats could only dream of becoming—or sucking face with. Possessed of a vivid beauty that extended beyond his pretty face through long limbs that could express a full vocabulary of dancerly and clownlike movements, Keanu was, not surprisingly, being written up—and pinned up—all across the country.

But the connection that audiences felt with Keanu went beyond his looks. In the late '80s and into the '90s, mainstream views of masculinity were held on a tight leash. Soft life skills like healthy and functional emotional expression were for girls (ew!) or, worse, gay people (double ew!). Men and boys of this time were taught to forsake vulnerability in the service of being, well, a "real man." This reality was painfully narrow and affected men, boys, women, teenage girls, and anyone outside the typical binary system of gender identification. Baby-boomer existential malaise combined nicely with AIDS-crisis-fueled homophobia to create a toxic landscape for personal growth and development in folks both straight and gay in the days of *Braveheart*, *Bad Boys II*, and *Friends*.

In a time when being an "average" teen truly blew chunks, being a teen with something to work on or discover quickly translated into being someone with something to hide.

Keanu, through his performances, was creating a living visual example of a young person with comfort in and control of a broader range of emotion and experience than the average adolescent off-screen. Whether he meant to or not, his fluency in feminine and masculine energies, and a combination of the two, was wedging open the slammed-shut window of gender roles in the Reagan/Bush era. Plus, he was gaining steady buzz, mega-crushes, and career traction. It was only a matter of time (travel) before such a promising young actor took a star-making turn.

Bogus Journeys

The first of Keanu's truly iconic roles, Ted "Theodore" Logan of 1989's *Bill & Ted's Excellent Adventure* is a triumph of doofy sweetness, held together with excellent comic timing and a hopefulness bordering on pathology. What could have been a snarky, cynical take on Idiot Kids These Days is, through Keanu's performance and partnership with Alex Winter's Bill, a portrait of an achingly sincere, strangely innocent pair of punks out to do good and eventually learn how to play their instruments. Ted, specifically, is a Gen X puppy trapped in human form. The role is what turned Keanu from "that guy in the movie with the troubled teens" into a household name.

But the role also solidified a part of Keanu's image that has never really disappeared: the idea that *he* is the doofus. We all can be doofuses, of course, but the doofus punishment here didn't fit the doofus "crime." Still, this less-than-generous image had to compete with the consistent emotional honesty of his onscreen work, particularly in Keanu's small but key role in Ron Howard's 1989 dysfunctional-family comedy classic *Parenthood*. The pain and plaintiveness he brings to the character of Tod, a goofy teen parent and husband, rings funny but true, especially in his monologue about how you need a "license to catch a fish but they'll let any butt-reamin' asshole be a father." Tod isn't just a repeat of Ted, even if the characters' hearts beat in the same excellent time.

Critics, while getting a kick out of *Bill & Ted* and *Parenthood*, started to see the forest for what they totally thought were, like, the trees. Keanu Reeves had the audacity to play a few teen roles in the '80s and '90s, in which he was required to speak like a teen of the '80s and '90s, so critics began to damn him as an *actual* teen from the '80s and '90s. Out of this perception came a critical shift: Keanu stopped being considered a talented, artsy, young thing and became an avatar of clueless, burned out, idiotic Gen Xers. By playing lucky idiots, the idea of him actually *being* a lucky idiot took root in the press and became a long-running cultural joke.

Allow us to use our gum to fix a broken part of this phone booth while we ponder a question for the ages . . .

Why Did the Critics Start Dragging Keanu Reeves to Hell?[1]

In the time between his career's illustrious beginnings and middles, Keanu acquired a rogues' gallery of critics and viewers who lined up for their chance to take a shot at his good name—a name that means, according to every article written about him, "a cool breeze over the mountains" in Hawaiian.

Armed not with throwing stars or those guns with really long silencers, critics took fierce aim with their words.

"Reeves is fundamentally blank and uninteresting."
—Peter Bradshaw, *The Guardian*, on Keanu Reeves in *Street Kings*

"The film's pretensions are rendered even more ludicrous by Keanu's lovingly detailed impersonation of a sleep-walking plank."
—Chris Tookey, *Daily Mail*, on Keanu Reeves in *Constantine*

"Such lines as 'Come, come let us thither' do not fall trippingly off this surfer dude's tongue."
—Peter Travers, *Rolling Stone*, on Keanu Reeves in *Much Ado About Nothing*

---

[1] With the exception of Roger Ebert, who always seemed to like the actor and respected a good many of his choices.

"With his stiff body language and wooden delivery, his every word falls like drops of flat Diet Coke rather than intoxicating wine."

—Lisa Schwarzbaum, *Entertainment Weekly*, on Keanu Reeves in *A Walk in the Clouds*

Liaising Dangerously with "Surfer Vibes"

If negative press is the curl of a wave, then Keanu was caught inside for a long time. As a teenager, he was an awkward interviewee, open and off the cuff without providing perfect sound bites. As an adult, he was reticent and irritable, though in fairness, some of the questions asked by interviewers were truly inane. But now that the 'ssance has taken hold, he is often thoughtful, thankful, and wise.

He has always been fairly private, with the exception of his early years in Hollywood, when he was apt to yap about his deadbeat dad or talk about his sadness over not getting certain parts, in the process alluding to a *possible* beef with Rob Lowe. (If you have information about this beef, contact us.) Keanu didn't make the press's job easy. He made it clear that he found it both surreal and annoying to have to sacrifice his private life to be a public artist. This perfectly normal but astoundingly non-movie-star-like attitude, combined with shaky performances in miscast roles, intensified the haterade.

Bram Stoker's Dreadfully Accented Jonathan Harker in *Bram Stoker's Dracula*

Maybe you think he was miscast. Maybe you think (as Keanu does) that he was just bad. Either way, critical response to Keanu's accent in this 1992 mall-goth magnum opus from Francis Ford Coppola definitely put a nail in the freshly constructed coffin of Keanu's acting reputation.

> "Contend with surfer dude Keanu Reeves' British accent."
> —Rod Lurie, *Los Angeles Magazine*, on Keanu Reeves in *Bram Stoker's Dracula*

Living to Get Radical

> "Johnny Utah. What a ridiculous, beautiful name."
> —Keanu Reeves

Kathryn Bigelow, the groundbreaking director and future Oscar winner for her directorial work on *The Hurt Locker*, had to fight to cast Keanu Reeves in his first role as an action star in the classic bike-robbing-surfer-gang thriller *Point Break*. This was the early '90s, and "The Ahhnold" was the biggest action star of the time. Putting a pretty-boy airhead into the role of a whip-smart cocksure FBI agent? Sounds about as crazy as sending that FBI agent undercover in a sting to catch a gang of bank-robbing, mask-wearing, thrill-chasing surfer bros looking for the ultimate high: life on the run!

> "Point Break makes those of us who don't spend our lives searching for the ultimate physical rush feel like second-class citizens. The film turns reckless athletic valor into a new form of aristocracy."
> —Owen Gleiberman, *Entertainment Weekly*, on *Point Break*

Point Break can be classified as utterly ridiculous, sure. But it hits notes of high-octane visceral emotion as well as high camp, all while riding the awesome power of Bigelow's unique and visually dynamic wave. This is due, in large part, to Keanu Reeves and Patrick Swayze waxing poetic while standing within kissing distance of each other's lush lips and ocean-sprayed faces. We hadn't dispensed with 'roid-bro norms in the early '90s, so seeing Keanu's Johnny Utah and Patrick Swayze's Bodhi interact so intimately scrambled a lot of signals. It made people feel a lot of feelings, some of them VERY good and some of them VERY uncomfortable.

But it also rang true. The desire to be close to someone who is close to their own pinnacle and *really* doesn't care about anyone else in their way . . . but kinda has a thing for you and can make you realize that all you thought you knew about life was naught but dust in the wind? Bad romance is a universal experience. Keanu visibly and totally allows Swayze's Bodhi to carry him away on the gnarliest wave without any macho or protective posturing to avoid seeming "girly" or "gay." Robbie Collin captured this intention perfectly in his retrospective review of the movie for the *Telegraph* in 2016:

> It's unlikely that a male director would have had the nerve for this—or that two more established male stars, with hard-won hard-man reputations to defend, would have thrown themselves into it with quite so much gusto. In a promotional interview, Swayze described the film as being miles from "slap-ass, macho, jokey crap. . . . I wanted to play it like a love story between two men." In 80s action movies, the male body is a weapon of war. *Point Break* turns it into a source of pleasure.

Keanu continued to embody vulnerability, even in his tough(er)-dude performances like Johnny Utah, tapping into a duality and fluidity within himself that has become an ineffable quality of his characters. He has refined this technique over his career, and it's a key reason he resonates with audiences, then and now.

I Will Change When Everyone Expects It the Least

Keanu dared to follow up his surfer-bro action movie with:
1. Gus Van Sant's queer masterpiece *My Own Private Idaho,* in which he tenderly breaks River Phoenix's heart while also doing experimental Shakespeare
2. *Bill & Ted's Bogus Journey*

And Then Die Hard on a Bus

In the 1990s, there were two distinct attitudes toward Keanu: beloved by fans and despised by critics. There were random, glowing write-ups, but roiling haters abounded—and in 1994 they had a field day with *Speed*. In this movie, Keanu played along with some of the expectations of traditional action-star masculinity—he went to the gym and got a haircut—but he wouldn't condescend to or ogle his very funny female co-lead, Sandra Bullock.

Critics seemed to buy into a very '90s idea of Jocks versus Nerds, and the mixed reviews of Keanu's performance in *Speed* reflect this. Many critics loved the film—it was directed by Jan de Bont, the cinematographer behind *Die Hard*—but others found the casting of Keanu suspect. Was he a Pretty Boy or a Jock? Was he dumb or was he smart? Hal Hinson of the *Washington Post* said this of Keanu's performance:

The real sex object here, though, is Reeves, who with his brush cut and pumped-up physique is barely recognizable as the loose, eager-puppy actor from his earlier films. As Jack, he reads every line as if he really, really cared, and though he's undeniably hunky and cute as a button, he's so earnest that he has no electricity, no life.

It's this dissonance between how Keanu looked—traditionally masculine—and the way he played the character—earnest and concerned, not cutting and quippy like Bruce Willis in *Die Hard*—that really got under critics' skins. The comparison couldn't be helped; *Speed* is, essentially, *Die Hard* on a bus (but better—fight us!). Keanu was sneered at for becoming an action star and, more important, for not leaning all the way in to action-hero stereotypes as they existed at that time. (Again.)

But his version of an action hero is something we needed then and are finally embracing now. He portrayed a hero and a team player with non-cynical earnestness, compassion, and respect for the people he shared space with—including women! Jan de Bont said of Keanu, "What makes him stand out is that he dares to let emotions show. He has a vulnerable quality—if you had a daughter, you'd let him take her out. A little old-fashioned, chivalrous. We've had enough cartoon-type action heroes." Culture, and specifically Marvel movies, eventually came around to this idea. But at the time, this was truly revolutionary stuff, poorly misunderstood as bad acting.

Follow the White Rabbit

Even as Keanu honed his craft and selected roles based on some secret algorithm known only to him, critics approached his career with the limited perspective that is (*gasp!*) often reserved for actresses. Keanu was often cheered for holding his own opposite actors who were better than him, credited for being watchable, and praised for allowing his beauty or blankness to do his acting for him. Basically, he was congratulated if he sat there and looked pretty. *Almost* like a woman.

The innovation and success of *The Matrix* granted him a brief reprieve from this kind of press. The movie was (and is) so singular and game-changing that long-time haters of Keanu Reeves were either stunned into silence, shocked into looking at him in a more nuanced way, or forced to double down, uncomfortably, on the old "lucky break" excuse. (Part of the mythos surrounding the making of *The Matrix* is that every other bankable actor in town had already rejected the role, most notably Will Smith in favor of *Wild Wild West*. At one point, the part was even offered to Keanu's *Speed* co-star, Sandra Bullock.)

But, as the sequels came out, praise for *The Matrix*—and Keanu—hit a saturation point.

"Neo continues to be a custom-made role for Reeves's limited talents. The fact that his one-dimensional character is dazed and confused throughout most of the film fits Reeves's performance style to a T."
—Paul Clinton, CNN review of *The Matrix Revolutions*

Chicks Dig Scars

As the millennium turned, critics continued to scratch at the irritation that was Keanu Reeves. Movies like *The Replacements* in 2000 and, a year later, *Sweet November* were seen as marked departures from the action movies he could, or should, be making after unparalleled genre success. They were panned accordingly, especially by the same critics and periodicals that rejected him as an action star in the early 1990s. The *Orlando Sentinel* said of *Sweet November*, "As Bill and Ted might say, it's one bogus journey, dude," proving that some references never get old. The subtext of such derisive reviews seemed to be: Does this guy age, and can't we leave him in the past? There was a simmering sense that Keanu had overstayed his welcome, that he should've aged out of the "real" reason people wanted to cast him in the first place: his beauty.

What does that say about the arbiters of taste in the '90s and early aughts? Well, suffice it to say, the loudest voices then generally belonged to older white men. Perhaps it's no wonder they didn't quite know what to make of a beautifully ambiguous dreamboat like Keanu. One reviewer even snarkily noted, in a take on *The Last Time I Committed Suicide* (1997), that audiences should brace themselves because pretty-boy Keanu was gone and he had grown a double chin!

One must wonder if the acidity of this hot take seeped into the public consciousness, playing a part in rough box office returns and, ultimately, declining studio offers.

Things were fairly quiet between *The Matrix* and *The Devil's Advocate*, after all.

> "More than a lot of actors, I think my public persona has really colored the interpretation of my work. . . . I think I've been pigeon-holed because of who I am or who they perceive me to be, or who I was."
> —Keanu Reeves, *Premiere* magazine, 2005

The Replacements

Careers aren't made by critics and studios alone. Even in the depths of the Keanu-hating years, his star remained constant . . . and solidly bankable. Critics might not have valued him, but audiences certainly did. And thanks to the internet, they started to disrupt the narrative and have their say online. The Empire writers were about to see the Empire readers strike back.

What began as GeoCities webrings grew into well-curated websites and endless message board archives dedicated to the exploration and appreciation of Keanu Reeves's career. Although Keanu is not active on social media, countless timelines are dedicated to exploring his work and/or archiving images of him lookin' bitchin' on a motorcycle. Memes and gifs are legion. These days, Keanu's refreshed career vitality seems reflected by his virality. The internet can be its own hellscape, but it has also provided a cozy common room for people to gather and examine what they love about Keanu now and what they've treasured about him all along.

I'm Thinking I'm Back

Our phone booth has made it back to our time. A time when we can consider the qualities that make Keanu Reeves both a good and fascinating actor as ones that we, as a culture, are finally starting to value again. A time when we find worth—rather than contempt—in vulnerability, flexibility, and fluidity. Our renewed interest in his playfulness, soulfulness, and ability to take down all the bad guys with a pencil is more than a feast of memes and a festival of thirst. Changing attitudes about male sensitivity have shifted the public's perception of Keanu from "ridiculous joke who got lucky" to an "underrated (inter)national treasure"—even though, admittedly, he's not so hot with accents.

That isn't to say those qualities are not under threat, even today. John Wick is a prince of vengeance and grief, and ours is a time of vengeance and grief as well. As that weighs on a people, they look for light and good things. They turn to the decency that has always been there and see it with the same loving eyes, or they allow for a thoughtful new view. None of us has a Continental Hotel we can escape to, right?

We just have the movies—and one another.

And it is up to us to decide if we will break the Matrix and live—in the Keanussance.

HOW DO YOU SOLVE A PROBLEM LIKE KEANU?

The topic of Keanu Charles Reeves is so surprisingly expansive, so filled with interesting twists and turns, that it would be impossible to cover everything in one slim yet Keanu-packed book.

However! There are several tasty Keanu nuggets that we've gleaned from internet round-ups, listicles, and slideshows. And so, in the interest of helping you crush your enemies at bar trivia nights, here are our favorite "Random Keanu Facts from the Internet."

- Keanu Charles Reeves first blessed the world with his glorious presence on September 2, 1964, in Beirut, Lebanon. He was born to an English costume designer mother, Patricia Taylor, and an American father, Samuel Nowlin Reeves, Jr.

- After his parents' divorce, his family moved . . . a lot, including to Sydney, Australia; New York City, and Toronto, Ontario. As a result, Keanu attended four different high schools in five years.

- Academically, Keanu says he was average but good at English and creative writing. He was on the chess team and was was such a successful hockey goalie he was nick-named The Wall.

- Keanu eventually won a place at a prestigious performing-arts school but was such a little rebel he ended up getting expelled at sixteen!

- But perhaps it was the pernicious influence of British Comedy that led the young Reeves astray. As the man himself says "I was raised on *The Two Ronnies*, *Monty Python* . . . I always loved the irreverence. Maybe it led to me getting that letter from school." We feel this is a solid theory and think the BBC should explain themselves.

- Keanu caught the acting bug—and Shakespeare fever—early. He played Mercutio in a production of *Romeo & Juliet* as a teenager. While it would be a minute before he would take up Shakespeare again, he did end up leaving high school to move to L.A. shortly after.

- Reciting Shakespeare out loud is a Keanu coping mecha-nism. Jan de Bont, director of *Speed*, got to experience such soliloquys in the middle of the L.A. freeway.

- Keanu once dated Sofia Coppola. There is photo evi-dence. They look hip as hell.

- When Keanu was young and acting in LA, he put his earnings in a laundry basket. He'd take what he'd need out of the basket and leave the rest for another day. We imagine his wealth management team is a bit more sophisticated than a wicker basket these days, but who is to say?

- Keanu is a perfectionist. He is known to shout profanities at himself and work tirelessly until he gets a take right when shooting.

- Keanu Reeves has described himself as "a triple threat Virgo."

- In 2010 in the UK, more baby boys were named Keanu than Jeffrey, Malcolm, Braden, Devin, Graham, Keith, Roland, Desmond, Emmett, or Roger. The name is particularly popular in London.

- Keanu Reeves waited patiently for twenty minutes in the rain to get into his own wrap party for *Daughter of God* because he was too polite to make a scene. After the mix-up, the club owner said, "I didn't know he was kept waiting, and he didn't say anything to me! He's a very relaxed person."

- Keanu wrestled with Alice Cooper as a kid. His mother was Cooper's costume designer, and when the rocker stopped by their home to visit, he challenged a young

Keanu and his friend to a battle. Apparently he didn't go easy on the boys and tied them into "a human knot," according to the friend.

- In 1997, Keanu was photographed hanging out with a homeless guy on the side streets of West Hollywood. They ate snacks, shared drinks, and Keanu laid on his back while listening to the guy's stories. This wasn't a PR stunt. This is just a thing Keanu *does*.

- He was the young guy in *Babes in Toyland*. You know, the '80s movie with baby Drew Barrymore. You may remember him, but did you remember it was *him*?!

- Other early jobs include sharpening ice skates (he was clearly eager to rack up Canadian cliché points), landscaping, and making a hundred pounds of pasta a day in a store called Pastissima. (He made it all the way to manager by the time he turned eighteen but quit for his first acting gig.)

- He was haunted by a ghostly jacket as a child. The phantom clothing floated into his room and he didn't realize it was real until he saw his nanny reacting, too!

- Keanu has dipped his multitalented toes into other parts of filmmaking. He directed the innovative *Man of Tai Chi* in 2013, produced the award-winning documentary *Side by Side* in 2012, and produced and starred in *Henry's Crime* in 2011. Evidently he wants the rest of us to feel bad about our slacker selves.

- Erwin Stoff, Keanu's first manager, is still his manager today.

- Keanu played Ortiz the Dogboy in the cult hit *Freaked* and has an uncredited cameo as a homeless man in *Poetic Justice*.

- For a God amongst Men, he's quite self-deprecating. "I'm a meathead, I can't help it, man. You've got smart people and you've got dumb people. You just happen to be spending some time with a dumb person."

- Despite the above protest, he can recite Shakespeare's Sonnet 30 from memory. He also turned down a part in Michael Mann's *Heat* (which eventually went to Al Pacino) to star as Hamlet in a stage production in Canada—after he finished shooting *Speed*.

- He reads voraciously, despite being dyslexic. This includes all 1,267,069 words of Marcel Proust's *In Search of Lost Time*, because apparently Keanu doesn't feel he is sad enough. While shooting *A Walk in the Clouds*, he took a hockey puck to the face. The poor lamb proceeded to complete a kissing scene the next day, with six stitches!

- He played the James Dean character in the remake of *Rebel Without a Cause*, which somehow serves as the basis for Paula Abdul's 1991 "Rush Rush" video.

- Keanu also played an on-and-off again hockey game for over ten years with strangers. "I saw some guys at a gas station once who had hockey equipment in their car, and I asked them what they were doing, and they said they were playing street hockey, so I asked them if I could play. So I became involved in a street hockey game that took place every weekend for over ten years."

- Not only does he still take the subway, he's been caught on camera giving up his seat to other passengers.

- A real Orthodox priest conducted the wedding scene between him and Winona Ryder in *Bram Stoker's Dracula*! This means, technically speaking, they're really married! If you squint really hard with your brain!

- At Dogstar's first gig, a little-known band named Weezer was their opening act.

- Of his musical skills, he says, "I'm the worst bass player in the whole world. . . . I have no rhythm." That might be because he's left-handed but plays the bass right-handed.

- You can see Keanu's yellow Fender bass guitar being played by Kim Gordon in the Sonic Youth video for "100%."

- The universe has tried very hard to kill Keanu, but he has thus far evaded the Grim Reaper's icy grip to the extent that we suspect *Bill & Ted's Bogus Journey* might have been a documentary. Injuries sustained riding motorcycles include a broken ankle, broken ribs, broken teeth, a ruptured spleen, and a memorable moment when one of the EMTs dropped his stretcher while loading it into an ambulance.

- Despite this history, Keanu loves motorcycles so much that he started his own business, the Arch Motorcycle Company, with a friend. They make custom superbikes that cost $78,000 each.

- Early stage names suggested by his agents, who thought his name was too exotic, include K. C. Reeves and Norman Kreeves. Keanu, who consulted with the ocean in a fit of existential despair, came back to them with Chuck Spadina. He got to keep his name.

- Fans trespassed on Keanu's property back in 1990. Instead of calling the police, he had a beer with them. (You can see photos on Reddit.)

- Keanu bought the Holy Shotgun prop from *Constantine* as a gift to director Francis Lawrence.

- When filming the *John Wick* nightclub fight sequence, Keanu had the flu and was running a 104-degree fever.

- Keanu's favorite phrases include "Good clean fun," describing things as "a hoot," calling people "cats," and answering press questions with "Today, I'll choose," regardless of the question.

- Keanu starred in the hit play *Wolfboy* as a youth in Canada and got major notice for the sexy photo poster displaying him kissing another man. His mother supervised the airbrushing of her son's acne in a power-mom move that has served us all.

- Keanu took a $2 million pay cut for *The Devil's Advocate* so producers could afford Al Pacino, and a reported 90 percent pay cut on *The Replacements* so they could hire Gene Hackman.

- Keanu was paid a proportion of the earnings for *The Matrix* and ended up getting $35 million after the film became a huge hit. When negotiating his profit-sharing deal for the sequels, However, he chose to give some of his points to the special-effects and behind-the-scenes teams. By some accounts, the total that Reeves could have earned but chose to distribute to the crew comes to over $75 million.

- Keanu has reportedly been secretly funding children's hospitals and cancer research from a private foundation.

- Keanu's love interest in *Point Break*, Lori Petty, has gone on record stating, "Oh, he's a very good kisser. . . . He's obviously very, very gifted. It's something you can't learn. He's definitely blessed, and he works very hard. . . . That's all you need: God's blessing, and lips." This last one is, admittedly, less of a fun fact and more something we wish to haunt your dreams. You're welcome.

- Keanu's mom created the bunny costume Dolly Parton wore on the cover of *Playboy* in 1978. A 19-year-old Keanu proudly wore the costume for Halloween, though tragically there are no photos of this blessed event.

- For such an easygoing dude, people just love suing Keanu. This includes a woman who claimed that he used hypnosis and impersonated her ex-husband to impregnate her. After a DNA test proved he was not the father, the suit was thrown out.

ALL THE KISSING WE CANNOT SEE

"There's no low stakes in romance."
—Keanu Reeves

Hollywood, you must atone.

For over thirty years, Keanu Reeves has been acting in movies. In that time, only a slender, shimmering slice of his filmography offers him as a true Romantic Lead.

A quick glance at most romantic leads of the 1980s and '90s—what could have been Keanu's leading love-interest heyday—makes us wonder why Hollywood ignored the haze of golden light around *A River Runs through It* (1992), *A Walk in the Clouds* (1995), and *In Love and War* (1995). More to the point: Why the hell didn't Hollywood give this man more kissin' work based on his beauty alone, not to mention his charisma and sense of humor? One must further wonder: Didn't Hugh Grant get tired? Wasn't Leonardo DiCaprio ever too busy? Was it never an option to skip over Tom Hanks?

Whatever the case might be, we look askance but content ourselves with the following films, whose casting directors showed some sense.

In the 2000 sports comedy **The Replacements**, Keanu plays Shane Falco, a man who thinks he can avoid future failures by hiding away on his boat and being beautiful all by himself. But you can't play football alone, Keanu. At least not for long. And it would certainly be unwise to play without heeding the wisdom of a lovely cheerleader, played by

Brooke Langton, who knows more about the game than anyone else on the field. While the love-story-within-the-redemption-story pans out with typical late-'90s cinematic ease, you can still feel the stakes—and the low-pitched attraction—as much as quarterbacks feel getting sacked. Also, the kiss between Shane and his Lady Love in her quiet after-hours bar holds a prominent place in the Slow-Burn Make-out Hall of Fame.

Another kissing scene worth noting is in 2006's romantic drama *The Lake House*. This lip-lock—a well-earned face grabber between Keanu and Sandra Bullock—takes place in a sun-drenched field in suburban Chicago. Our heroes have weathered a very specific time-travel conceit as well as their own hang-ups to arrive at said sun-drenched field. The movie is thoughtful and melancholy, and it scares us all with a high-stakes timeline-convergence scenario, only to ultimately reward our valiant efforts of tracking through with our heroes for a kiss that is both luscious and lovely, in addition to being the likely prelude to the creation of a long line of beautiful brunette children.

Yet there's more to romance than pants feelings and mutual respect. There's also a deep and noble responsibility to do what is right for someone else—especially when that person is hot. *A Walk in the Clouds* (1995) tells the tale of a young soldier returned from war to a fractured marriage (she applies for an annulment to be with another dude; it's fine) and a curious set of circumstances. While out looking for work, he ends up meeting a high-class Mexican

American graduate student as beautiful as he is, but she's pregnant by her professor. And wouldn't you know it, that professor wants nothing to do with her now that she's in the family way! Keanu offers to pose as her husband for a night and smooth things over with her traditionalist father. *What will happen?* you ask as you watch this gorgeous film play with family dynamics, grape crushing, and love growing despite the odds. *Will they kiss?* you wonder. Yes, though the kissing is not even a little bit as salacious as one might hope. Still, this is good, and in the words of Keanu, "to play someone who cares and wants to give is very cool."

And this is really the most of it. Come on, Hollywood! What are you waiting for? He may be immortal, but we are running out of time!

Honorable Mentions

In addition to the above list, we have a bunch of also-rans and weak contenders. We're including them here because we are extremely thirsty and living in a kiss-lite, Naked-Keanu-free Sahara. (Thanks, Hollywood).

***Dangerous Liaisons* (1988):** *Everyone* is naked in this movie. Which makes it extra rage-inducing that they stick Keanu in the deep, blurry background.

***Point Break* (1991):** He's a romantic lead for two different characters, but he only makes out with one. This is a tragedy for which we will never forgive Kathryn Bigelow.

Sweet November (2001): We will forget that this movie ever happened, though Keanu and Charlize Theron are very pretty in it.

Destination Wedding (2018): No offense to this film, but we wait forever to get a Keanu rom com, and what we get is *Destination* Fucking *Wedding*???

Siberia (2018): Maybe this counts as a romantic lead role for those who occasionally sell diamonds in Russia. And maybe there is some absolutely scintillating shoulder touching during an illicit make-out session. But this film, though interesting, gives us merely a smattering of dirty diamonds. We want a big-ass rock.

Always Be My Maybe (2019): It's played for laughs, but Keanu's kisses with Ali Wong in between the pair's whispers of sweet, intense nothings have likely enjoyed as many replays as Randall Park's "I Punched Keanu Reeves" rap. You're on the right track, Hollywood! Took you long enough.

PART II

Keanu and Race, or Why Keanu Reeves Is the Goth Audrey Hepburn

Oh, I see it a little around the eyes . . ."

Keanu Reeves was not Western pop culture's first white-passing Eurasian sleeper agent. We'd had them before: Vivien Leigh and Merle Oberon for example. And we would have them again: Hailee Steinfeld, Mark-Paul Gosselaar, and even Rob Schneider.

But Keanu was different. He was hiding in plain sight. He kept his name (with the

exception of a short-lived blip as white-bread K. C. Reeves) and with that came the inevitable discussion of his background. During many a chat show interview and in many a breathy teen magazine profile, the public was informed that his unusual moniker, courtesy of a white English mother and a mixed Chinese Hawaiian Portuguese father, meant "cool breeze over the mountains" and was surely a sign that baby Keanu was destined to be dreamy.

But at the time of baby Keanu's birth on September 2, 1964, his parents' marriage was illegal in six U.S. states. It would be another year before laws restricting immigration based on nationality, which targeted Asian immigrants, were struck down. In addition, Asian representation in Hollywood during this time period was, well, about what you would expect.

This is the era of the yellowface roles that everyone is properly embarrassed about now, Mickey Rooney in *Breakfast at Tiffany's* being a well-known but sadly not unique example. Even if played by an Asian actor, Asian men were depicted as sexless, effeminate, sinister, inscrutable, and basically the last kind of person you'd want to stumble upon in a dark alley, let alone bring home to your mother. (George Takei's Hikaru Sulu on *Star Trek* was a rare exception.)

Unsurprisingly, there were few well-known mixed white/Asian actors working when Keanu was growing up. Those who made it were often cast in stereotypical roles, like Nancy Kwan, or were forced to make their movies outside of Hollywood, like Bruce Lee. That is, if they looked noticeably Asian to Western audiences. Meanwhile, white-passing Eurasians, like the aforementioned Merle Oberon and Vivien Leigh, kept their mixed backgrounds under close wraps so they could play the leading roles that were de facto reserved for white performers.

Things had improved a little by the time Keanu started

his career in the late 1980s. Sure, some of the old racist and stereotypical parts still lingered (though by then they had an outside chance of being played by an Asian actor, such as Long Duk Dong in 1984's *Sixteen Candles*). There were finally positive Asian role models in Western media, but, for the most part, those characters were more Asian than Asian American.

In movies and TV shows like *Mulan*, *The Karate Kid*, and *Big Trouble in Little China*, you can find badass Asian characters, but their backstories are all about CHINA/JAPAN/KOREA (and sometimes HONOR, but mostly CHINA/JAPAN/KOREA). These idealized and exoticized stories didn't really reflect the experiences of children of the Asian diaspora, including Keanu. The lives of second- or third-generation Asian Americans, when represented at all, were often confined to Very Special Episodes and typically seen through the eyes of white characters. The "Hell Money" episode in the third season of *The X-Files* is a good example of this World Within a World, in which Mulder and Scully are the audience's proxy into a mysterious community populated by Asians, to be viewed from the outside in. Asian stereotyping was soon replaced with a different problem: Asian tokenism. The '80s and '90s saw the rise of the ONE Asian character with a speaking role or the ONE Asian member of an ensemble team. From *Power Rangers* to *Jurassic Park* to *Captain Planet* to *Die Hard*, these characters were strong, they were smart, and they held their own. They were also never, ever the lead.

So how did Keanu pull off becoming a successful leading man in an era of swole Schwarzeneggers and cocky Cruises? Well, the most obvious explanation is that, like his biracial predecessors, he passed as white to a Western audience. The roles he was landing—the naif in period pieces, FBI agents, lone cops trying to take down evil Dennis Hopper—were gigs offered almost exclusively to white actors (and Will Smith). His character in *Street Kings* is even racist against Asians, for Neo's sake.

Still, there's something more about Keanu's stardom that set him apart from these macho manly leads. It isn't just that he showed a gentleness and sensitivity that was unusual in an action star (though that is certainly true). It's not as if he was the only actor in the late '80s and early '90s with a special knack for playing vulnerable with a secret toughness, or tough with a secret vulnerability; River Phoenix and Johnny Depp were great at it, too. This combination of sex appeal and angst was perfect for the sensibilities of the *Nevermind* generation, whose own take on masculinity was only just emerging from a dusty Baby Boomer–shaped cocoon.

But what was unique to Keanu's stardom was the specific *way* that his vulnerability was depicted: at times almost as feminine. In many ways, the true points of comparison are not other male leads but his contemporary female costars. The camerawork in such movies as *Point Break* and *Little Buddha* (1993) linger lovingly on his body with the same suggestiveness normally reserved for starlets, following the gaze of other characters as they consume him with their eyes. In these movies, he is a figure to be watched just as much as he does the watching, yet still within the framework of a traditional male role.

The specter of the effeminate Asian man trope might have lurked behind such creative decisions, but those portrayals traditionally used feminization as a misogynistic means of undermining a villainous character. Here, under Keanu's watchful gaze, the trope has been inverted and elevated beyond the old comical or grotesque portrayals, perhaps by sheer dint of his magnetism, in service of his heroism. Even today, Asian men are rarely cast as the love interest, though there are a few notable exceptions. (Henry Golding, whose British charm offers him a recognizable way into potential movie stardom, Steven Yeun in *The Walking Dead*, and Manny Jacinto in *The Good Place* are a few.) In the early days of Keanu's career, however, the Asian male dreamboat was essentially nonexistent in Western culture. Maybe that explains the bewildering tendency of '90s filmmakers to cast one of the most stunning men ever captured on camera as the rejected suitor, one who loses out to such swains as a badly bewigged Gary Oldman and an elderly Jack Nicholson. The cinematography of these movies clearly portrays Keanu as babetacular, but the narratives can't seem to make logical sense of the idea that someone ambiguous in so many ways could be a woman's first choice. It's as if the filmmakers couldn't quite put their finger on what to do, and so they kept returning to strange echoes of racist Hollywood tropes.

The media begrudgingly acknowledged that Keanu's

ambiguity might be a big part of his sex appeal. Early pro-files, including *Vanity Fair*'s "Kabuki Keanu," leaned into this ambiguity hard by featuring our man in '80s Goth club makeup, brooding for the camera. (A headline and creative direction that would be a no-no today, certainly.) Yet as night follows day and blockbuster movie follows thought-ful think piece, the (mostly straight white male) culture writers of the time Did Not Get It. To the media, he was a talentless and wooden male bimbo. ("Those exotic chops are patently not in receipt of electrical impulses from the brain in the conventional manner," wrote Peter Bradshaw in a particularly scathing review for the *Guardian*.) And that's even before the persistent homophobic whispers about his personal life. These "whispers" were a fancy version of "Lol, gay." They were also not unlike the slightly queer-coded ways in which Asian men, from Charlie Chan to Fu Man-chu, had been portrayed and belittled in Western film. But while these thunderous dismissals spoke to higher ideals of Taste, they seem, in hindsight, yet another way to emascu-late and undercut Keanu's appeal according to the messed-up mores of the day. (Keanu, to his credit, was one of the few stars who behaved like an adult when confronted with gay rumors in the '90s. "People were saying that David Geffen and I had gotten married and it just blew me away. Not that they thought I was gay, but that they thought I could land a guy that hot.") Nevertheless, here he was, in the thick of it, making blockbusters and prestigious literary adaptations with the best of them—and in the lead role to boot.

And while Keanu was playing sexy havoc with traditional male roles, something similarly confusing was brewing throughout the late '80s through early '90s with regards to female representation. Tempering the gains made by feminism with the conservatism of previous filmgoers, casting directors were especially fond of casting an eye back to the Golden Age of Hollywood, But Now With a Feisty Modern Twist. This is something demonstrated in the slew of Goth Audrey Hepburn wannabes that came to prominence in this era, from Winona Ryder to Helena Bonham-Carter to Natalie Portman. (The Jewish starlets grouped together in this Exotic-But-Not-Too-Much pigeonhole is an essay in and of itself.) And to be sure, these actresses had something about them that evoked the same ethereal beauty mixed with girl-next-door energy of peak gamine Audrey. They weren't exactly her, per se, but they were close.

But none of them captured the same combination of relatable yet otherworldly, of being known yet unknowable, as much as Keanu. The true Goth Audrey Hepburn successor was there all along, taking almost the same wide-eyed roles (admittedly with extra blood and explosions). We all just missed it because he was a guy.

Allow us to explain. Both Keanu Reeves's and Audrey Hepburn's down-to-earth enigmatic appeal has been put to good use by filmmakers. Both actors have a knack for emoting through silent expression and artless gesture. Even without laying everything bare, they give us a mainline straight into their emotions. As a result, both are the ideal audience ciphers. You might go to a George Clooney movie to watch him be George Clooney, or a Will Smith movie to watch him be Will Smith, but with a Keanu Reeves movie, you go to see *yourself* be Keanu.

It is this connection to the audience that makes both actors the perfect fish out of water, able to move between worlds without becoming the Other. This is true of Keanu's defining roles (*Bill & Ted, Point Break, The Matrix*) and Audrey's (*Roman Holiday, Funny Face, Sabrina, Charade, My Fair Lady*). As they move through the world of the movie, their experiences are our experiences, and their emotions become our emotions.

But their thoughts are not necessarily our thoughts. A familiar trope in their movies is the sudden out-there decision—one that comes completely out of the blue for the audience but makes perfect emotional sense the moment it happens. You can probably call to mind some of Keanu's characters' impulsive momentum-shifting actions, including shooting Santino in *John Wick 2*, shooting himself in *The Devil's Advocate*, and shooting the air while screaming in homoerotically charged frustration in *Point Break*.

Audrey's roles, on the other perfectly gloved hand, are notably less trigger happy; her characters are more prone to suddenly running away from an unhappy situation. (See: running out of a New York City taxi in the rain in *Breakfast at Tiffany's* to look for her cat or running away from a palace in a drug-fueled stupor to Experience Real Life in *Roman Holiday*). Still, as both movies involve a lonely protagonist's life circumstances changing as symbolized by embracing and officially adopting a pet, in many ways John Wick is really just an extremely violent Holly Golightly. They even both have a certain way with sleek black tailoring.

In other words, it was Keanu, with his beautiful sexual, gender, and racial ambiguity, that is the true Gen X heir to the Audrey Hepburn throne. It is perhaps this very ambiguity that allows a wider range of people to see themselves in him, and put themselves in his shoes. And no movie has tapped into that better than *The Matrix*.

Keanu might not have been the first choice to play Neo (that would be Will Smith), but he was still perfect for the story's enigmatic hero. *The Matrix*, like most cyberpunk fiction, is heavily influenced by Asian pop culture. This, unfortunately, can play out in a problematic *Blade Runner* "techno-orientalist" way, in which the world is full of Asian culture but zero to few characters of Asian descent. *The Matrix* neatly sidestepped this problem. Mixing Hong Kong kung-fu movie action, a traditional *sifu*/student plotline, and big Hollywood special effects, the movie is a hybrid of cultures that aspires to more than mere set dressing. By hiring Chinese trainer Yuen Woo Ping and mixed-race actors Marcus Chong and Keanu, Asians were brought back into a world that leans heavily on Asian imagery.

With his features that could pass as white but still read as slightly "exotic," in the parlance of the press, Keanu was a perfect avatar to ease mainstream Western audiences accustomed to white leads into the universe of the story. In an inversion of old Hollywood, the bad guys in the Matrix franchise are interchangeable white men, and the good guys are the minority-majority misfits, the Children of Zion. The titular Matrix is populated with mainly white characters and coded in shiny, big-city, first-world privilege. Meanwhile, "reality" is post-apocalyptic and multiracial, with shades of the cities and regions that have been left to rot in the real world. Keanu, with his ethnically ambiguous looks and everyman otherworldliness, could exist in and between two worlds, focused on but set apart from both.

The story famously opens with a binary choice: blue pill or red pill, fantasy or reality. From the get-go, Neo must choose between these two states, with no space for liminality. From the first movie, in which Keanu gives an iconic Bruce Lee nose tap as he throws down with Laurence Fishburne in a VR dojo, to the final movie, where he's able to move between the two worlds at will, Keanu is the embodiment of what it means to merge two disparate worlds into one identity. His universality is, well, universal.

The Matrix also marks a sea change in the way that minorities and mixed-race performers were portrayed in the media, which certainly picked up on the appeal of diversity in the late '90s and early aughts. Accordingly, in the post-*Matrix* era, references to Keanu's background kicked up a notch. "He's the face of globalization: Born in Beirut to an English mother and a father of Hawaiian and Chinese descent, he's a citizen of the world. And unlike the multiracial Vin Diesel, he saves the universe with geekiness, not mere muscle," gushed a 2006 *Wired* article. He even played roles that were explicitly (in the case of *47 Ronin*) or implicitly (in the case of *Man of Tai Chi*) mixed race. A 2003 *New York Times* article entitled "Generation E.A.: Ethnically Ambiguous" pegged movie stars like Vin Diesel and Jessica Alba as the exemplars of Gen Y (ye olde term for Millenials), the most ethnically diverse generation in American history. Mixed-race models and actors were valorized for their differences and for reflecting the "changing face of American beauty," in accordance with "the new reality of America."

But mixed-race people are nothing new, including in the movie world. People have been migrating between regions for millennia, and when people come together, they will inevitably get busy. Keanu wasn't even the first mixed-race member of his family, let alone the first mixed-race Hollywood A-lister. It's just that mixed-race stars of previous eras were allowed to be the lead only if their non-white heritage remained firmly in the closet. The one difference for this new generation of performers was that what was once a liability had become marketable, identified as trendy by the *New York Times*.

What was unusual about Keanu in the early days was that he was openly mixed race but still cast in roles usually performed by white actors. His fame served as the turning point between Asian Americans as sidekicks and Asian Americans as leads. In the wake of his rise came such A-listers as Lucy Liu, John Cho, Steven Yeun, Constance Wu, and Henry Golding. Now, Asian men could be stoner bros (*Harold and Kumar*), the likable everyman who comes into his own and gets the girl (*The Walking Dead*), the "My Daughter Is in Peril and I'm INTENSE" dad (*Searching*), the cute best friend the teenage heroine realizes she was in love with all along (*Edge of Seventeen*), the goofy point-of-view kid character (*Up*), and even the sexy love interest (everything Henry Golding has been in). Keanu was no mere Eurasian sleeper agent. He was a full-blown Eurasian Trojan horse.

So what is the future of Asians in Hollywood after Keanu? Well, we aren't out of the woods yet. Movies like *21* straight up rewrote the real-life Asian Americans on whom the story was based as white, and white performers are still sometimes cast in Asian roles. But where this practice was once painfully normal, people are coming around to the idea that erasing Asian people from their own stories might be a bit on the fucked-up side. As frustrating as it might be to have Emma Stone cast as partly Hawaiian Chinese in *Aloha*, or rewriting Major Kusanagi as Major Killian to accommodate Scarlett Johansson as the lead in *Ghost in the Shell*, it at least sparks major discussion and criticism. Today, Asian American kids have more role models to look up to than Keanu did growing up in the 1970s and '80s. There are major syndicated sitcoms like *Fresh off the Boat*, blockbuster movies like *Crazy Rich Asians* detailing the Asian American experience from the inside. Mixed-race kids now even get to see explicitly mixed Asian characters (such as the protagonists in *Big Hero Six* and *To All the Boys I've Loved Before*) actually played by actors of Asian descent instead of the brown-haired white actors favored in the past (looking at you, *3 Ninjas*).

The most important aspect of these characters is that they are fully fleshed-out humans, with wants, needs, and desires that are just as important as those of white characters. They have personality traits beyond being "Asian." Their background might come up as part of their backstory, or it might not be relevant. It's a small step forward, but it's a start. And perhaps, in some way, we have Keanu Reeves to thank.

KEANUSPIRACIES

Despite, or perhaps because of, being such a private star, the world is rife with Keanu Konspiracies. After all, just what does the man *do* between funding children's hospitals, starting small businesses, or starring in critically acclaimed blockbusters? Surely there must be something else, some hidden darkness we're not seeing?

People have inevitably filled the gaps with their own explanations. So here, in our most sensible and not at all wild-eyed manner, is a list of conspiracy theories for the enigma that is Keanu Charles Reeves.

KEANU IS A VAMPIRE: It happened on the set of Bram Stoker's *Dracula*. Winona Ryder, Anthony Hopkins, and Sadie Frost were also bitten, which is why they all look exactly the same as they did in 1992!

KEANU IS IMMORTAL: His image has been recorded for centuries, which you can track on keanuisimmortal.com (seriously). He's wise beyond his years. When asked point-blank, even the man himself did not deny it. And who has time to read as much as he has? Immortal guys, that's who.

KEANU IS A TIME TRAVELER: See above, but swap in a science-y explanation instead of a supernatural one.

KEANU IS D. B. COOPER: In 1971, an unidentified man hijacked a Boeing 727 aircraft, extorted $200,000 from the

FBI in exchange for the lives of his hostages, and parachuted to an unknown fate without being noticed by anyone onboard that plane or on the planes tailing the hijacked jet. We think he used the money for extensive plastic surgery, went to Hollywood, and then re-created that very scene in *Point Break*.

KEANU REEVES IS MAN-MADE GLOBAL WARMING: Because he's just so dang hot.

KEANU HAS PREDICTED THE END OF THE WORLD: Through a series of specifically timed blinks in the opening scene of *Sweet November*, Keanu has secretly gifted the world with the exact date of the apocalypse. Unfortunately, no one has yet deciphered this code, so the day remains undetermined.

KEANU IS HEAD OF THE NEW WORLD ORDER: The Illuminati has been renamed the Keanuminati in his honor. Jay-Z is reportedly pissed.

THERE HAVE BEEN SEVERAL KEANUS. THIS IS JUST THE LATEST ONE.: The original Keanu's real name is Cummerbund, and he has been living like a king on Prince Edward Island off the proceeds of every Keanu movie until *Little Buddha*. The second lived briefly and was disposed of not long after *Johnny Mnemonic*. The current Keanu is our fifth.

KEANU IS THE ZODIAC KILLER: It's always the nice ones.

DRESS FOR SUCCESS:
CHOOSE YOUR OWN TURTLENECK

Keanu Reeves is known for being both chill and chilly. He also knows that the trick to keeping a cool head starts with having a warm neck. Find your own Keanu Turtleneck Alignment within these signature looks.

1. Black Turtleneck with Black Sunglasses and Optional Floor-Length Pleather Priest Coat (*The Matrices*)

You value practicality, which makes the wipe-clean properties of pleather ideal. You'd be amazed by the stains you get taking down dystopian virtual realities.

2. Tan Turtleneck with Fox-Brown Blazer (*The Lake House*)

You work hard but prioritize warmth and style in equal measure. Still, you long for love, and one day you hope to replace the embrace of your favorite corduroy jacket with the arms of Sandra Bullock. Until you find her/she saves you from the past that is her future, you'll continue to beat loneliness at its own game by layering on responsibilities at work as well as some autumnal coordinates.

3. Black Turtleneck with Shadow-Gray Mosca Suit (*John Wick*)

You have committed countless sins, but not being sartorially savvy isn't one of them.

4. Black Cashmere Turtleneck
(*Something's Gotta Give*)

Look, you know you're a catch. But you're also magnanimous as hell and don't like to rub your perfection in everyone's face—even such intelligent, refined faces as some pretty, spectacularly aging playwrights. Black cashmere is the look of refined beauty; it really brings out the kindly glint in your eyes and the plushness of your lips, always slighted parted in the start of a smile that you know will soon end in a kiss.

5. Mock Turtleneck with Waistcoat
(*Bram Stoker's Dracula*)

Sure, this is technically just a white button-up with a high collar, and ironically it doesn't come with vampire-deflecting abilities. But what better choice to sell "Uptight Englishman Abroad" than a good old-fashioned throat strangler? Similarly strained accent not included.

PART III

"You Working Again, John?": The Incredible Work Ethic of Keanu Reeves

Don't think you are. *Know* you are."

These words are spoken by baby Laurence Fishburne (age 38) to an even babier Keanu Reeves (age 34) as the two prepare to rise up and break the Matrix. The "knowing you are" part happens with rela-

tive quickness for Keanu's Neo, since it takes only about twenty minutes to download the greatest hits of human combat skills into his brain. That moment when Keanu opens his eyes and says "I know kung fu" is the envy of all modern viewers who are still waiting for an I Know Kung Fu app.

But a glitch can happen when we expect "knowing we are" to come easily, instantly, or, at the very least, automatically, without spending the time working and hacking away at what we care about. The desire to "know we are" is as timeless as Keanu's face. People long to be good at things— to learn, to grow, to excel, and to demonstrate what they have gleaned from experience and experiment alike. Even to be known for it. That's why YouTube tutorials and Skillshare are so popular. But putting in the time? Well, wouldn't it be much nicer to wait for the right app to come along? In a culture that pays lip service to the idea of hard work, we seem more attracted to the Effortless and the Natural rather than the try-hard success stories. We love smart people but we don't love nerds. We parade the show pony and leave the workhorse in the barn.

Keanu Reeves is a workhorse who looks like a show pony.

Has he managed some truly creative dressage? Yes. Has he stumbled publicly while attempting feats of glory (i.e., certain accents)? Also yes. Keanu has definitely been a half-bad or just-plain-bad actor; he has also been a good—even great—one.

Because Keanu knows what we know, too: You better work.

Keanu on a Workhorse in Times Square

"I've heard Anthony Hopkins say this, but acting really is like painting—the craft and skill of it. The way that you act is a lot like the way you work the paint, and the more you do it,

the more you know it. That's what I love. A good day on the set—creating the work, the piece—is a hoot."
—Keanu Reeves

Keanu Reeves works with what he has, and he works to get better with what he's got.

You often hear actors described as "brave" or "risky" for making creative choices or for taking leaps of faith with unknown directors or off-market stories. Keanu is the first to admit he's made some "wacky" shit—his filmography zigs and zags more than that of any other actor we can name—but every director and co-star he's worked with readily admit he does so with unwavering interest, commitment, and concern—for the performance he gives, the story he's telling, and the filmmaking as a whole. He isn't just out to shine his own star. He's out to share a pocket universe by, in the parlance of Keanu, "making a good picture." The late great Philip Seymour Hoffman, had this to say about Keanu's acting style and work ethic:

I don't think there's anything Keanu doesn't know. I heard he went and played Hamlet at some theater once, and I see the things he does, and it's like, he's just another actor struggling to try to get better. And I am, too. I just don't get into that "he's someone to put down" kinda thing. Acting's a really hard thing to do, after all, and some people, I think, do it easier than others. But I do think that some people get better, and I also think some people take it very seriously, and I have a feeling he's somebody who probably does, that he struggles like everybody else to try to do it well. But if I saw him, I'd probably ask him for tips, to be quite honest, my friend. I'd be like, "So, how did you get in that first Matrix movie? How'd you swing that?"

You can't make a good picture without working hard. And you definitely can't make one on your own.

No One Gets Off the Bus

There's a nebulous way that critics and participants in pop culture praise successful leading actors. A truly successful lead can carry a film, in the sense that they serve as the viewer's analogue onscreen—albeit a hotter, stronger, smarter version. Landing the trick doesn't always have to do with smoldering beauty or undeniable charisma, though. The essential element of a leading actor's watchability, believability, and bankability is usually attributed to some magical and mysterious aspect of star power. When it comes to Keanu, that ineffable quicksilver quality is present, certainly. But his star power has a backup generator: technique.

It wasn't unusual for profiles of Keanu to mention his commitment to the Stanislavski method or his love of Shakespeare—these references were as frequent as reminders that *keanu* means "cool breeze over the mountains" in Hawaiian. But this 1994 *Newsweek* piece, entitled "Goodbye, Airhead," pays respect to the acting craft of the man who was about to drive into a different strata of stardom with *Speed*, which is still so delightfully exciting and well made that it's hard to believe it's twenty-plus years old.

Before you race to Google (or even Bing) to look up what the hell Stanislavski or *An Actor Prepares* is all about, just know that the key tenets of the Stanislavski system require an actor to get their role across as naturally as possible. You might be more familiar with this as method acting (examples include Heath Ledger never breaking character on the set of *The Dark Knight* or Christian Bale starving himself or bulking up for roles). The basic idea is to take a natural and motivated approach to both your role and the story. Basically, to play make-believe super, extra hard.

Stanislavski's approach is essentially the LARPing of the acting world, and the practitioners of this acting style can lead successfully because they are embodying their roles, using empathy and action. Logic follows that the lead then makes room for the characters/actors they're interacting with to be fully embodied as well. This way, the leading actor is not siloed into their own journey of epic, showboating solitude. Via the guiding light of Stanislavski's teachings, the true lead can join the ensemble's merry band, widening the scope of the story they're all telling. Star Power +1000XP.

While *Speed* could easily have been *clears throat* *his* vehicle, Keanu worked to make every scene partner feel like a true co-lead for the duration of that scene. Keanu only gets into the damn bus around the forty-minute mark, and by then he has already shared top billing with Jeff Daniels, a host of coworkers you literally don't see again until the end of the film, and a guy whose car he commandeers on the L.A. freeway.

When we finally do meet our true co-lead—that wildcat-behind-the-wheel Sandra Bullock—we're suddenly watching a duo so dynamic that their chemistry alone guaranteed studio funding for *The Lake House*.

During a promotional interview for *Speed*, Keanu was asked what he thought of Sandra Bullock. "She has such a wonderful energy about her, and light. She really gives and wants things to be . . . springtime. And she's a really great actress, too. . . . She's been fighting the direction of damsel-in-distress."

This interview is then interrupted by a literal hug-fest between Sandy and Keanu, which serves as a freaking adorable illustration of Keanu's well-known reverence for his co-stars. This moment translates directly into the believability of their chemistry onscreen.

That chemistry is, at least in part, enabled by Keanu's classical approach and generous spirit, which feels more characteristic of a strong supporting actor than a leading man. He makes space for the performances his co-stars are giving by watching their faces, which is an effective way of building and maintaining dramatic tension, both within the scene and between the viewer and the film. His eyes focus our eyes. We look where he looks. We see what he sees. We care about what he cares about. In making space for others, he creates a unique physicality for his own character that communicates that character's objectives, biases, and desires.

Send in the Clowns

At first blush, a role can seem clear cut in its simplicity (dumb kid, good cop, bad guy), and it could be easy for the actor to make a quick judgment call and phone in a lazy performance. But Keanu works to treat his characters with the same thoughtful and engaged approach that he uses with his co-stars. Many have charged Bill S. Preston, Esq. and Ted "Theodore" Logan for being as dumb as kids come, but when asked how they approached Bill and Ted's intelligence in a special episode of the Shout!Takes podcast, Keanu and his co-star, Alex Winter, opened up about working hard *not* to take their dudes at face value.

KEANU: I always found them kind of perhaps not school smart, but certainly intellectually and emotionally super open and available, but in a way where they're supposed to always face challenges and overcome them. And I think they do that in the kind of fool's journey.

ALEX: I never really saw them as dumb. They exhibit a lot of curiosity . . . emotional depth . . . they are immature.

KEANU: But what's a dumb person? I mean, what is that? They're hopeful.

ALEX: Dumb wasn't how we came at them.

KEANU: They almost have this kind of reaction to being defeated or down. Like, of course they can go talk to Death, because they're the ones that can. Or, we can time travel. Of course we can save the world.

Scott Kroopf, the producer of *Bill & Ted*, seemed to be in awe of Keanu's approach to what could've been treated as an easy role.

> He brought to it an oddly serious sensibility for such an unserious character. That was part of what made the movie great and it's also what makes Keanu great as an actor. You'd walk into his trailer and he'd be reading Stanislavsky's [*sic*] *An Actor Prepares* and applying it to Ted. The reason he ended up unfairly taking this rap of "he IS Ted" was that he did such a great job and it's hard for any actor, when they truly excel in something, to break out of it.

Keanu Reeves, Power Virgo

If you want to know exactly what kind of worker Keanu is, look no further than his directors and line coach.

> "Keanu—the guy just won't stay down. He commits fully. And he has bad days like all of us, there's days he can't even touch his toes. But he won't quit, he'll just switch modes and go, 'Ok, I'm here, what can I do that will improve me?' And he listens, he's collaborative—he's a freak."
> —Chad Stahelski, director of the John Wick franchise

> "You care about Keanu. He's a big-hearted guy. There were a lot of passages in German and he had them all translated.

He was always digging deeper. Keanu's the kind of guy who would call you up about it at two in the morning."
—Richard Linklater, director of *A Scanner Darkly*

"I had no idea he was going to be that involved in what he was doing. Keanu made the part much more than it was, and much more than I thought it could be."
—Sam Raimi, director of *The Gift*

"If I sent him a book that had something to do with the film, he would read it right away. Keanu would read *City of Night* and then he would read three other books by John Rechy. And River would, like, not look at the first page of the book.
—Gus Van Sant, director of *My Own Private Idaho*

"He arrived having learned it from beginning to end, every single solitary word that *Hamlet* has to speak and most of the other characters' words as well. It amazed me how easily he could pull out quotes from other characters in the play to reference back to his own. His knowledge was encyclopedic, not only of *Hamlet* but also of other Shakespeare plays and of the revenge tragedies which were the bases for *Hamlet*."
—Richard Hurst, Keanu's line coach for *Hamlet*

Keanu Reeves is a big reader. Interviews are stuffed with mentions of books he's reading for roles, for pleasure, or for big ideas to inform his participation in, as he puts it, "the bourgeois rat race" of being a Hollywood actor. He takes notes, he keeps notebooks, and he recites Shakespeare off the cuff to A) get better at it and B) mitigate stressful situations, like being mobbed by crowds of superfans. In a Reddit AMA from 2014, he noted some of his favorite books—*The Count of Monte Cristo*, *The Lord of the Rings*, *The Idiot*, *Notes from the Underground*, *The Brothers Karamazov*, John Updike's Rabbit series—and some of the authors he'd been reading recently: Don Delillo, William Gibson, and Philip K. Dick. He has famously read all of *In Search of Lost Time* by Marcel Proust.

His entire tricky-to-trace career trajectory is fueled by a desire to always get better, learn more, and have a new tool in his kit. He's mentioned his workaholic tendencies and "Virgo-ness coming out" more than once. He has shadowed exorcists and heart surgeons, street kids and the FBI. He's studied with Buddhist lamas, vocal coaches, and even a Zippo lighter trainer. He's learned dance moves, foreign languages, and fighting styles. This isn't merely chat-show fodder or an interesting way to populate the "personal life" section of his Wikipedia page; he continues to master the tricks of his trade and ways of the world to serve the stories he's telling and the characters he's playing. Some actors beef up or slim down to pull off a role, and Keanu is no stranger to such physical alterations. But he's more interested in exploring the psychology of his characters; for him, the best way to do so is to understand why their minds work while working to construct the bodies those minds ride around in.

"He wants to win," Keanu said of Johnny Utah, his character in *Point Break*, in an interview with the *San Jose Mercury News* in 1995. He continued:

> The essence of football, especially for a quarterback like he was, is to win. He has no concept of what that means except from a football "win" mentality. But all of that gets torn apart. He gets confronted with moral questions. To get to Bodhi, he manipulates a girl in an evil way. But it's from innocence, almost. His innocence about the game of winning.

For a guy who likes to reference the phrase "your greatest enemy is your greatest teacher," it sounds like one of his most significant learning experiences was delivered by some gnarly waves. Reeves learned to surf for the role of Johnny Utah, and he told director Kathryn Bigelow that he was going to train in an area of Hawaii that she knew was way above his pay grade. "I started out a month and a half before filming, went on a surfing trip to Kauai with a friend, and I got slapped! I mean, the first time I went into the water, the board just smacked me in the head." Kathryn appreciated his dedication, but even more that the experience of getting "slapped" humbled him. It was good for the role. "But eventually, I could do it," says Keanu. "I could stand up, depending on the wave."

I Don't Know Kung Fu

"The best way to fake being good is to be good. There's no way around it. When you see Keanu sliding a car, that's Keanu sliding a car. That is not something you can learn on the day. That's twenty years of his life spent racing motorcycles and drifting cars and rally sports. When you see him do judo it's 'cause he spent a phenomenal amount of time doing it. When you see that video of him shooting, that is not normal. That is competitive shooting level. He is not faking it. So we go with that. We get our guy to be good, which makes our character good, which allows me to shoot in certain ways. Out of respect for me, he trains twice as hard to give me creative choices. If it's the other way around, my creative choices aren't made out of creativity, they're based on getting it through. They're forced edits."

—Chad Stahelski, director of *John Wick*

Keanu Reeves refuses to state that he knows or has studied martial arts. "I know movie kung fu," he says with a laugh in interview after interview. But he does admit to the benefits of a classical education, to having good teachers, and to life-changing experiences that set him on the questing path to have more, ready to find the next story to tell, whatever it might be.

As it turns out, a story that shaped this approach to life and filmmaking found him: *The Matrix*.

It's hard to believe, in these post-*Matrix* times, that

Asian martial arts used to be a rarity in Western film. The Wachowski sisters had different ideas, but when faced with the dearth of American stunt artists who could produce the high-finesse set pieces they imagined for their game-changing opus on altering reality and living truly, they brought in the legendary Hong Kong stunt specialist Yuen Woo Ping. He agreed, but on one condition: the cast must train specifically with him to learn kung fu and work with the wires. No matter how long it took.

A tall order. "We sat around discussing the philosophy and the metaphors of the script," the Wachowskis would later say. "We knew it would take a maniacal commitment from someone, and Keanu was our maniac." They were right.

In the end, Keanu spent four months of exhausting eight-hour days training for the role. He learned kung fu as a novice, including how to apply the techniques to wires, and incorporated intense physical conditioning. The preparation was so hardcore that it aggravated on old neck injury and required surgery. Keanu's reaction to months of physical torture? "It was an honor to work with Woo Ping. . . . I've always been a fan of his work and it was a wonderful opportunity to learn." *The Matrix* might've portrayed Keanu as absorbing kung fu in mere minutes, but the reality is that he worked his ass off learning the old-fashioned way, with no shortcuts. It's this openness and enthusiasm that has allowed Keanu to become one of the greatest stars of his generation, action or otherwise. And it's his insane work ethic that has turned him from lanky kid into convincing onscreen badass, and all manner of characters in between.

The Matrix may start to glitch when too many programs work at once. But in our real world, we can try to be as good as Keanu is at our own version of Movie Kung Fu. If we work at it.

And get good.

HERE'S JOHNNY: A QUIZ TO DETERMINE WHICH KEANU-JOHN YOU ARE

Keanu has a knack for playing the Everyman, and the Everyman has a knack for being named John. Tally your answers to discover the Keanu-John most closely aligned to your soul.

1. **A machine appears to whisk you through time to ensure that you pass your history class. You:**

   A. Use it to go back to med school instead of elite super-assassin school and specialize in rare diseases. All of them.

   B. Watch it sullenly for any sudden movement while smoking your ninth cigarette that hour.

   C. This! Needs! To! Be! Brought! To! The! F! B! I!

   D. Prod it to deduce what manner of device this is. You're sure nothing could go wrong!

   E. Finally, you can enact that needlessly complicated nefarious scheme you've always wanted to try. You know, the one with the goats.

2. **The woman you love lives two years in the future, and you can communicate with her only through a mailbox at your father's lake house in the Chicago suburbs. You:**

   A. Stare at it in beautiful, moody anguish, perhaps while casually garroting someone to pass the time.

   B. Know well enough not to trust messages from the beyond. You leave the Chicago suburbs forever, never stopping to wonder what might have been.

   C. Wait for her, knowing that nothing, not even sociopathic former friends, can stop your love.

   D. Write polite daily missives about your thoughts on the queer customs of the locals, why they cross themselves in your presence, and why that eccentric old man keeps on stopping by to stroke your neck.

   E. Decide to ruin her chances at love with any other by staging elaborate trickery to besmirch her good name.

3. **Your friend dispassionately confesses to killing his girlfriend and shows you and Crispin Glover her body. Crispin Glover goes into hysterics and makes everyone promise not to narc. You:**

   A. Kill the killer and put his body on display. Kill the guys who come to take it down. Put their bodies on display, too. Stand back. Admire your artwork.

   B. Do a quick check of literal Hell to see what's up with this guy.

   C. Narc like hell. You work for the F! B! I!

D. Place a tender hand upon the killer's shoulder, look him square in the eyes, and attempt to detect if his soul was moved by himself alone or because of a manipulation by an evil man who takes what he wishes from the world, whether he is granted permission or no.

E. Smile. Thou shalt use this for blackmail later.

4. Strange things are afoot at the Circle K. You:

A. Nod, grimly.

B. Laugh, mirthlessly.

C. Stare, longingly, and with a pent-up desire which you are only beginning to comprehend.

D. Stutter, nervously.

E. Flee, quietly.

5. You learn you are The One. You:

A. Were, once. Now you just want to retire.

B. Know. And you hate it.

C. Thought so, and you wish you could go skydiving with a special someone to celebrate.

D. Gasp! Really? You can't wait to tell your girlfriend!

E. Know. And thou dost love it.

6. Your local NFL team is on strike, and a strike team is being assembled to make the play-offs. You:

A. Are pressured via a blood oath (that you tried and failed to get out of) to kill them all, with a pencil.

B. Smirk. People always have such a problem with their heroes being switched up on them.

C. Make heart eyes at the coolest member of your new team. The one with the messy blond hair and Zen philosophy. He seems totally trustworthy and is probably your new best friend!

D. Are not sure what to make of these American ball sports but shall give it a jolly good try all the same.

E. Hire someone to knife the striking team whilst they carouse in a bawdy house. Now YOU are the team! And you alone! Mwahahaha!

7. You are trapped on a bus that will explode if it drops below 50 miles per hour. You:

A. Drive the bus, spare the innocents, kill the bad guys.

B. Start smoking. You always hated the bus.

C. Yesss! This is what you were trained to do! You are going to look so cool! Though, obviously, resolving this dangerous situation is what is most important to you. *Ahem*.

D. This is really beyond your comprehension. And you've spent time with vampires.

E. Sit back, relax, and watch thy monstrous plan unfold.

8. Your ability to never lose a case gets you hired at a hotshot law firm in New York City, where you learn the literal Devil is your father-boss. You:

A. Have faced worse. Papa doesn't last five minutes after your discovery.

B. Sigh with resigned exasperation. This explains everything.

C. Check if the Devil's face is really a mask—this has Bodhi written all over it!

D. Shudder to your core. Why can you not escape these immortal fiends?! Those who would drag you to the very pit with their wretched desires?!

E. Are delighted.

9. **Your best friend confesses his love to you with delicate awkwardness, for you both know you have only platonic feelings for him. You:**

A. Silently embrace him with a gentleness you have exercised previously with only your wife and dog.

B. Tell him the only thing you love is this noodle shop you went to one time, hold his gaze for a tender beat, then break the moment sharply by offering up one of your smokes.

C. Realize your platonic feelings run far deeper and truer than anything you've ever known, and you feel more thrilled than when you're in the Tube.

D. Smile politely and burn with confusion.

E. Enjoy the moment, then leave him in Italy when your father dies and you stand to inherit.

10. **You must coach a ragtag group of youths to a sports victory to pay off your gambling debts. You:**

A. Train them in the way of the gun and the sword. The other team won't see it coming.

B. Train them to defend themselves against the Forces of Darkness. There are things that are more important than some dumb game.

C. Train them with ruthless efficiency on the field, and make sure every line is filled out on every sheet of their homework, goddammit.

D. Train them to play like gentlemen on and off the field, as this is the best way to prepare oneself for the rigors of life.

E. Train them to do your dirty work. The people of the city truly felt that you were safe to care for their youth? A-haha! The fools!

YOUR RESULTS

MOSTLY As: You are JOHN WICK

The Saddest John

MOSTLY Bs: You are JOHN CONSTANTINE

The Maddest John

MOSTLY Cs: You are JOHNNY UTAH

The Raddest John

MOSTLY Ds: You are JONATHAN HARKER

The Vlad-est Jon

MOSTLY Es: You are DON JOHN

The Baddest John

AN IMPOSSIBLY ROMANTIC MUSICAL STARRING KEANU REEVES, CHARLIZE THERON, AND WINONA RYDER

> "I want to make an impossibly romantic musical. . . . Now maybe it would need to be an older man's story. About love, and loss . . . and Paris."
>
> —Keanu Reeves on *ID10T with Chris Hardwick*

Let's imagine that musical for him.

JOHN WICK, CHAPTER 7: JE T'AIME

OVERVIEW: All current and former high-caliber super-assassins are granted one week of vacation as reprieve from their ultraviolent and hyper-stylish lives. **John Wick** takes his in Paris because he (and his new dog) has never seen the French catacombs. While in line for the catacombs, he meets another high-caliber super-assassin, **The Valentine (Charlize Theron)**, also taking her vacation. Soon we discover that The Valentine is actually the disguise of Agent Provocateur, a high-caliber super-cop hell-bent on being the one who brings Wick in.

AP will stop at nothing, even bringing along her bookish assistant, **Margot (Winona Ryder)**, to psychologically profile John Wick into a hell of his own making. But Margot has fallen for the man she understands so well from her studies, and when the two unite they form a bond as strong as the one John shares with any dog. That bond will be put to the test in a final showdown and a final *final* showdown . . . in Paris.

ACT I

"Paris Is for Lovers, Not Me"

John Wick soft-shoes through the slick streets of rain-swept Paris with his dog, looking for love but knowing he won't find it.

"Catacomb with Me"

JW meets The Valentine in line for the catacombs. They strike up a conversation about being married to the job, and when she is called away before they can enter the catacombs, JW is left to wonder if instead of finding love, maybe it . . . has found him?

"Trimming ze Wick"

The Valentine, as her true self, Agent Provocateur, sing-monologues about her plans to destroy John Wick for her own personal gain and pleasure. Her bookish assistant, Margot, is distressed. She has grown fond of the man she has profiled for so long and cannot bear to see him struck down by a bloodthirsty detective going rogue for glory.

"Un Chien Déjà Vu"

Keanu sings a ballad to his new dog about his old dog. First love is always first love, but new love is still love. Just different.

Margot: Are you comparing your love for someone new to your love for your dog?

John Wick: No. That was literally about my dog. But I think I could love again, too.

Margot reveals the truth about her research and AP's plans. They share a kiss and fall in love.

"In Love in Paris"

A big ensemble song, centering on JW and Margot in love, planning to leave their old lives behind and start a new one somewhere, in Paris.

John Wick: I never thought it would happen to moi, a kiss on the steps of Montmartre.

Could I really be yours? Beneath the dome of Sacré Coeur?

JW sings about how he could do his job in Paris and how

Margot could get a new job in Paris. Parisians sing about how they're annoyed by all the tourists in Paris. All sing about how they are in love in Paris.

"Catacomb Away with Me (Reprise)"
Agent Provocateur interrupts by taking out most of the town square and kidnapping Margot.

AP: *If you want to save her, meet me where we first met—
    the catacombs!*
JW: *We actually met in line for the catacombs—*
AP: *Damn you, John Wick!*

ACT II

"It's a Trap"
In an exclusive dance club hidden in the depths of the catacombs, Margot is nowhere in sight, but AP has gathered all of JW's enemies and some random French people to fight him to the death!

"Gun-Fu for Love"
A dream ballet where JW makes quick, poetic, and violent work of the club and fights his way out from the literal underworld and to the real final showdown at the top of the . . .

"Tour d'Eiffel"
AP sing-monologues about killing Margot and wounds JW before he can save his love. Margot, in turn, saves JW from

getting killed to death by pushing AP off the tower.

Margot: I gave her a beautiful death . . . that she was psychologically prepared for.

JW and Margot stumble across the plaza at the base of the tower and collapse in a heap amid the glow of the carousel. There, John's dog trots up with a pair of blood-spattered train tickets to . . .

"Provence (Finale)"

Love wins the day, and John Wick wins another international bounty on his head. Margot and John Wick are untroubled as they plan their new life, in love, in Provence.

FIN

PART IV

Keanu's Most Excellent Adventures in Collaboration

Take 1:
A lone figure in a well-cut suit under dramatic rainfall looks out into another neon-lit night of impossible achievement. He has just done The Things, and all of them well. All while looking like the gods breathed life into diamond-flecked granite instead of clay.

All while being tragically, truly, essentially *alone*.

Take 2:

A lone figure in a well-cut suit under dramatic rainfall looks out into another neon-lit night of impossible achievement. He has just done The Things, and all of them well. He has his partner to thank, really, and the last ten years they spent training to do The Things. Plus the first employee they hired when they finally cracked that five-year mark, when people saw one of their Things and said, hey, those two are starting to really get the hang of those Things. That employee brought a lot to the table at the noodle place they all went to for lunch on Fridays, and the person who brought them noodles had been a real game-changer when they started sharing their ideas about The Things. They all had to work double-time to keep up with Noodle Friend in those days. But that was how everyone learned. *Grew.* Now they all did The Things. Plus dreamed up New Things. Eating noodles all the while.

Keanu Reeves has played his fair share of Take 1 roles in the movies, but in reality he's a Take 2 dude in creative pursuits, both on and off the screen.

Plenty of movie stars build potent myths and box office returns via personas staked on being the only hero on their own individual journeys. Keanu is a different make of movie star. His collaborative spirit makes him a different make of maker, entirely. And he's got the successful dog-avenging action-movie franchise, the book publisher side hustle, and the bespoke motorcycle company to prove it.

But we're getting ahead of ourselves.

In addition to making life on Earth bearable, collaboration is key to any creative pursuit. From a distance, it can be easy to see good collaborators as mystical, mythical beings who just sort of emerge, fully formed, on the horizon of great deeds and successfully completed projects. But being a good, and real-life, collaborator involves resourcefulness, patience, and resilience to navigate the delicate dance steps of using passion to drive yourself and others to a common goal while checking your ego (and possibly rebuilding or reining in other egos) in the process.

Collaboration involves not only bringing your own skills and talents to the table but also learning to prize and develop the skills and talents of others. You have to give off energy and feed off energy, working from the idea that the best idea might not always be yours, but the best ideas are worth the same investment and investigation that you would bring to your own. It is a foxtrot, an epic road trip, a marathon, and a whole bunch of other extended metaphors that we could mix for days.

While the phrase "teamwork makes the dream work" is an eye-roller, teamwork really does . . . make the dream work. The development of so-called soft skills, like communication, listening, and sharing, paired with an ability to buckle down, open up, double up, or switch gears while keeping the shared vision of making A Really Great Thing, makes Keanu a versatile and effective collaborator.

Sometimes he works with long-time friends, sometimes with those whose skill sets and celebrity eclipse (or pale beside) his own. Whoever the partner, he takes stock of their gifts, respects their time, and brings game to meet game.

Of course, we aren't positing that Keanu Reeves was born pretty *and* ready to make friends and influence people. Maybe part of him was, and part of his drive to create with others outside the system is self-preservation in an industry that has, for his entire career, flung its door wide open for him—when it wasn't being slammed in his face.

One successful example of collaboration knocking that door off its damn hinges is Keanu's work with Chad Stahelski, co-director (and now sole director) of the John Wick franchise.

Keanu met Chad, as he has many of his current collaborators, on the set of *The Matrix*. Chad was Keanu's stunt double and a rising star in action design. Perhaps sharing a body as "The One" in the movie helped the two form a bond in the real world. Learning the ways of the other on set and in life enabled them to develop a friendship and professional partnership built on a dedication to craft and a desire to use action for bigger, better, and stronger storytelling.

Cut to twentyish years later. The script for *John Wick* crossed Keanu's path and he immediately thought of his former stunt pals, Chad Stahelski and David Leitch, as the perfect fit for the film's action design. But as he has told countless eager interviewers, he also secretly hoped the two men would want to direct.

They did.

It was the first time for both Stahelski and Leitch in the first-unit director's seat rather than the stunt-car driver's seat.

Keanu's work didn't end once he had the team locked in to direct. That was when his real collaboration began: spending months weighing in on creative aspects of the script, lending production assistance, and training so hard that "Keanu tactical videos" are practically their own subgenre on YouTube.

Ultimately, the film grossed $86 million against a $20

million budget, carrying the collaboration forth into *John Wick 2* and beyond. Stahelski said to Den of Geek in 2017, "I don't think the script was ever written; we wrote scenes, we wrote acts. It was a very slow and arduous process, but it was very fun . . . everyone authored everything."

That shared authorship has resulted in scores of fans eager for any and all chances to welcome back Mr. Wick, again and again.

High-octane action filmmaking with a global audience in mind is clearly a field that demands collaboration, but what of stylish and thoughtful art books?

Yes, reader!

X Artists' Books, or XAB, a publishing company based in Los Angeles, was founded by Keanu and his friend and compatriot in arty exploration, the visual artist Alexandra Grant. Their partnership began when Keanu wrote another friend a a poem, a delightful paean to self-care and sadness entitled "Ode to Happiness." While it started off as some-thing to make their friends laugh, Alexandra, a visual artist interested in language, pondered the piece for months. She then created visual art to complement the text: she hand-stitched her creation into a beautiful book for her friend.

This shared joy led to the decision to extend their bookmaking magic to another poem written by Keanu, "Shadows." In addition to making their own books with a shared history and sensibility, they seek out the work of emerging and fringe voices to create IRL experiences of pleasure, language, and visual art.

They also sought expertise from the German-based art book publisher Steidl, which was a shared source of inspiration. In a 2016 *W* magazine interview, Alexandra explained, "We can spend a lot of time debating. . . . Like, 'A raspberry hue? And should it be darker?" We can get obsessive."

Growth and obsession: the bosom buddies of happy collaboration!

In a *New York Times T Magazine* profile of the new business endeavor, Max Lakin noted:

> Hollywood is lousy with actors' vanity projects and left-field dalliances—burger joints and artisanal tequilas and cultish lifestyle companies that may or may not be pyramid schemes. But Reeves's extracurriculars feel more in sync with his persona: They're rooted in artless sincerity, whether he's playing bass and supplying backing vocals for the mid-90s alt-rock band Dogstar or cofounding a California motorcycle manufacturer called Arch. Instead of feeling like a departure from acting, these projects—along with bookmaking— express a genuine interest in not just creating objects but in the process of creation itself. "Not that we're reinventing anything," Reeves says. "But the idea of a quality book is definitely our ambition."

Now these publishers are working to create a beautiful, thoughtful stable of work by seeking out new collaborators, known and unknown.

"He's a wonderful artist, remarkable, epic. And he's all that as a person. And he's really mentored me through life." This sounds like something any of Keanu's co-stars may say about him, but is really Keanu Reeves speaking about Laurence Fishburne on *The Talk*. Keanu is famous for being a bit awkward and reluctant to talk about his finer qualities in interviews, but the praise pours forth when asked about his costars and collaborators. The appreciative attitude Keanu takes toward his co-stars might play a key role in how so many artists enjoy working with him time and again.

Sandra Bullock, Winona Ryder, Charlize Theron, Laurence Fishburne, and Peter Stormare are just a few of Keanu's frequent onscreen collaborators. Of course, actors don't always choose their co-stars, let alone choose to work with them in multiple films and franchises. Much of casting is up to zeitgeist, budgets, and sheer luck of the draw. What is unique to Keanu's repeat casting with certain co-stars is the sheer joy expressed by those co-stars at the ability to work with him again.

You can't swing a cool breeze over a mountain without hitting a celeb profile or interview featuring a co-star of Keanu's commending how good a man and generous an actor he is. Generous, in actor-speak, usually means that as a scene partner, Keanu not only gives his all—he works with his fellow performers to provide the support needed for them to be able to give their all. The cliché of the spotlight-greedy actor exists for a reason, so no wonder being "generous" as an actor gets highlighted by Keanu co-stars from the highly recognizable to the up-and-coming.

In fact, when Sandra Bullock was up-and-coming, she had this to say about Keanu to an on-set interviewer during the shooting of *Speed*: "He works so incredibly hard. It's rare that you get a fellow actor who says, you know, 'Is there anything else that I can change for you, would you like me to do something, what is it that's not working for you, can I change something?'"

"I can't explain in words why Sandra and I have chemistry on screen or why we work well together," Keanu told *Entertainment Weekly* when the two teamed up, years after *Speed*, to make *The Lake House*. "We just do, and I'm glad because I like her tremendously as a person. I always enjoy watching her work. She is funny as all heck, smart as a whip . . . it was great to have some life under our belts since the last time we worked together."

That life under the belt—and perhaps in Keanu's case a YSL belt—is something magical and mundane that makes these re-team-ups powerful. We get to see something onscreen informed by a relationship and trust established and developed off-screen. It deepens the dynamics on-screen. "Keanu was my first film partner. Prior to that I had been in supporting roles but in *Speed* I was really part of a team. I have a great affection for him," Bullock told interviewers in the production notes for *The Lake House*. "We've never lost track of each other. The minute we started rehearsals for *The Lake House* it was like coming home. It's an understanding and trust you cannot explain. You can tell because we argue all the time!"

Winona Ryder has also worked with Keanu on several films and had a hand in his being cast in *Bram Stoker's Dracula* when the studio passed on Johnny Depp. She was a direct factor in his being cast in *Destination Wedding*—she sent him the script and asked if he would do it—and her joy at working with him is apparent in every interview and bit of promotion the two did for the film.

During the press tour for *Destination Wedding* Winona gushed about her love for Keanu to *TODAY*: "I've had it forever, but now people are finally seeing it. Even though we're in character," said Ryder. You can sense it is born of a personal connection, but a professional appreciation and championship is also there. When asked by *Vanity Fair* about their collaboration, Winona said, "It's like what Katharine Hepburn said about Spencer Tracy. 'There's no embroidery. He just does it.' Which is so great. A lot of people embroider a lot." Keanu, of course, took this in bashful stride and responded, "I know, but there's some beautiful embroidery."

Trust and chemistry are tricky elements of a successful pairing on- or off-screen. How do you define what makes it work? Maybe you can't. Maybe that's just the reward of being open and present in life: you forge bonds with people who want to keep strengthening that bond as time goes on. As far as magic goes, collaboration falls hard on the practical side. When we look at successful co-workers like Keanu Reeves from the distant outside, it can feel like straight-up lucky magic. The kind that takes no work, no effort, all grace and uncontrollable circumstance. Taking a closer look at Keanu Reeves and his work, we see that his track record of joy is at least in part because of his dedication to finding the joy and making those movie moments we treasure really sing.

"I have a joy for life and I think I really centered in on it for Ted," Keanu told *Premiere Magazine* in their "Finding Neo" piece in 2005. "He's so nonjudgmental. He wants to see the best and is really alive in the best way. I don't know, he's in grace."

This kind of grace can go far in becoming a good collaborator. Work and a touch of perfectionism can go the rest of the way.

"I'm a Virgo, I like tasks, I like puzzles, I like trying to get good at something," Keanu said in a recent *John Wick 3: Parabellum* sneak peek video. Common, Keanu's *John Wick 2* co-star, experienced this firsthand when shooting a tough scene that neither actor felt they were getting right. Keanu pressed to retake over and over, and both men were exhausted. Keanu's dedication kept Common inspired. "There were times when it would feel like, 'Man, is this is ever going to work?' And when we finally got it, I just remember Keanu saying, 'Doesn't it feel good when we get it right?' I was like 'Yes!'"

Graham Yost, the screenwriter for *Speed* (and showrunner for TV's *Justified*) said that when he was creating the role of *Speed*'s hero, Jack Traven, he was interested in creating a character who wasn't perfect, but was good at "figuring out the trick." When speaking about the twentieth anniversary of *Speed* to *Entertainment Weekly*'s Mandi Bierly, Yost said:

> "My whole premise, basically, is that heroes in literature aren't necessarily the fastest, the smartest, the strongest whatever—but they're clever and they figure out the trick. They figure out how to beat the bad guy, not just through strength or even by being more intelligent, but just by being something that the bad guy doesn't see. And that's Perseus with Medusa and the shield. So I wanted Jack to be one of those guys who's able to figure out the trick."

Keanu is one of those guys who has figured out the trick of working well with others. Over and over again.

A great ship asks deep water, and in a true collaboration, you might be the water or you might be the ship. If you're collaborating with Keanu Reeves, you can change up the metaphor: A great motorcycle asks for open road. Both are needed for the adventure. As is persistence.

Yes, we are going to ride this metaphor to the end of the line, just as Keanu did when partnering with L.A.-based motorcycle architect Gard Hollinger to create Arch Motorcycle Company.

Keanu had to talk Hollinger into this collaboration. He was initially turned down when Keanu tried to commission some uninteresting custom work on one of his bikes. The two subsequently developed a friendship built on a mutual obsession with and appreciation for well-made motorcycles. They worked together to create a dream prototype while Hollinger was at his previous company, Chop Rod. All the while, Keanu pestered his new friend with his passions and dreams to start a company that would turn their fantasy bikes into realities—very expensive ones, granted, but beautiful creations designed to provide the perfect ride.

It took some doing. As Hollinger told Petrolicious in 2016, "Finally, I remember him saying, 'You know, I have listened to all these reasons why we shouldn't do this. Can you tell me some reasons why we might want to do this?' I thought that was interesting." Now, many years and several Squarespace Super Bowl commercials later, Arch Motorcycle Company makes some of the best bespoke bikes on the market, and it has had a profound effect on both men. In interview after interview, Hollinger has credited Keanu's passion for reigniting his own joy of riding. As for Keanu, he told Hotcars.com, "Someday we aren't going to be here, and it would be really great to leave something that matters to us, something we love."

Being a true collaborator demands the best of ourselves. To share our joy, to be playful and curious and passionate and patient, and to open our eyes to what we could make together is a gift we can give to ourselves, each other, and the world beyond. Leaving something we love after we're gone is a dream that we, and Keanu, can all share.

A RIVER (PHOENIX) RUNS THROUGH IT

Keanu Reeves and River Phoenix knew each other from when Keanu co-starred in the 1989 movie *Parenthood* with Martha Plimpton, a gifted actress and girlfriend of River's. The boys struck up a friendship on the set of Lawrence Kasdan's *I Love You to Death* (1990) and made movie magic and history with their performances in Gus Van Sant's *My Own Private Idaho* (1991). From reading their interviews and seeing their work, you immediately sense a deep-running simpatico that makes River's death—when both were still young—all the more heartbreaking.

River was the more articulate and propulsive of the two, and Keanu was his counterbalance. The friends shared an intimacy and a joy for the lives unfurling before them. In these early days of Keanu's career (and the middle of River's) they finished each other's sentences, boosted each other's confidence, kept each other's egos in check, and made plans for their friendship, careers, and futures.

Sandra Bullock once commented that she had never met anyone like River, with his kindness, honesty, and off-the-wall statements. But upon meeting Keanu on the set of *Speed*, Bullock said, "Oh my God, he's exactly like River."

An issue of *Interview* magazine in 1991 features the boys getting excited about acting in a Shakespeare play together. Keanu suggests that it would be a "hoot" to do *Romeo and Juliet* with River. "I'll be Juliet!" River agrees. There's a small collection of photos of them together from this time, and though neither can ever be called plain or unattractive on their own, together they are beautiful. They shine.

This connection and shared creative energy is something they carried from their friendship into their screen work: especially to the painfully true and delicately distressing campfire scene in *My Own Private Idaho*. The campfire scene. Oh, the ache and bloom and burn of it. Quoting this scene would be like flattening a butterfly between the pages of a book. So sorry, butterfly. We'll describe it instead.

River's character, Mike, haltingly confesses his love for the friend he knows does not love him back, Keanu's Scott Favor. Scott listens to Mike, follows his train of thought, holds his tongue . . . and then holds Mike close. In what could have been a moment of abandonment or revulsion, Scott lets Mike break his heart but holds him closer afterward and pets his hair. Scott's romantic rejection of Mike isn't designed to be cruel, just matter-of-fact. The scene's dialogue, silence, and attention paid plays into the brutally, beautifully awkward wrench of it all.

River and Keanu rewrote this scene from Van Sant's initial idea that the boys would never have clearly defined sexualities or romantic love for each other. The original intention was for the characters to suck each other off out of boredom in the desert. River had a notion and worked it out with Keanu, using little scraps of lines on paper and improvisation to bring what is largely considered the beating heart of the film to life. Together.

Some time after River's death, and as Keanu's own star shifted in different directions, another journalist asked about his friendship with River. After a long silence, Keanu expounded upon River's virtues before responding, "Where is my Juliet? Bullshit! Fuck! . . . He was a really good guy."

THE BALLAD OF KEANU:
A FANFIC

Tales as tall as The Stranger himself were told up and down ole California way back then. Tales about a young man, well known and well liked, who just up and *left* for a couple of years.

And to do what? Well, few folks know for sure, but that ain't stopped other folks from talkin'. You've maybe heard somethin' of his deeds—stories told 'bout a travelin' man, with keen eyes and kind hands, on a motorcycle and a mission to be exactly where he was needed.

All the way from La Jolla to Big Sur, folks were whispering about the new hero. They said The Stranger was as big as a barn and as strong as ten broncos lashed together. That he once jumped out of a plane without a parachute to pursue a no-good desperado and lived to tell the tale. That he once saved a bus full of innocent folks from certain doom. That he had traveled through time and faced down death. They even said that he had won a battle of wits with the Devil himself.

A lot of old hokum perhaps, and you might question the feller that their recollectin' of the young hero sounds too far-fetched to be true. But that's before he points out the scar on the face of a man who won't tell you how he came by it, or he mentions the fence out back that was mended by a tall dark stranger and marked with only **KR** carved into the post.

"Has Keanu been here?" you might ask. And while some folks might look like they wish to tell you, most times they'll look at you enigmatic like and say something along the lines of, "Maybe he was, brother, and maybe he wasn't. Who knows fer sure?"

Truth be told, there's only been a few folks willin' to go on record about exactly what they saw during those curious times—and even then, that takes some doin'. In fact, there's only one soul I know personal who was there and will give you his story straight.

You might feel doubtful, but as Billy the Barkeep refreshes your glass of rare Aussie red, you catch a glimmer of truth in his eyes (and a framed Dogstar shirt behind the bar). Could it be he possibly knows somethin' . . .of *What Keanu Reeves Did in the Two Years Between Filmin'* The Devil's Advocate *and* The Matrix?

HE COULD.

Billy Hawkins is a man now, but he was just a boy when .The Stranger rode into town. There wasn't much that marked him from anybody else, asides the fact he was real handsome and as silent as a subway station gunfight in *John Wick 2.*

That didn't matter none, and all eyes turned to him as

he parked his bike, paid the meter, and walked across the old town square that fateful day. Sure, the man might have been quiet. But even if you didn't know exactly what he was thinking, you somehow knew deep down in your bones just what he was *feeling*. And what he was feeling, Billy knew, was a mighty hankering for Justice.

The Stranger walked on over to Billy and flipped back his jet-black hair courteously.

"Little dude," he said, as Billy nodded back. "I hear tell that there are some unrighteous folks operating round these parts. Folks that have made it their business to make business out of other people's misery. And, well, that makes it my business to stop it."

Billy knew there was just one fellow that The Stranger could have meant: old Bobcat Joe McGrew, the scourge of Damnation, California! Why, right now, old Bobcat Joe was in a fit of stitches, afore he had presently thrown his favorite throwin' axe at the one-room schoolhouse and broke it clean in two!

Luckily, the schoolhouse was empty at the time, but unluckily, the children were all crying out in the yard, for their missed educational opportunities and because it looked like their teacher, Miss Everleigh, would be the next target.

"You just try it, Bobcat!" Miss Everleigh spat. And it looked as if he would!

"I won't if ye jest marry me!" Bobcat spat back.

Miss Everleigh spat back even harder. "Not even if Napoleon himself came down in a big ol' time machine and commanded me to," and with that she yelped as the mangiest rascal this side of the 101 grabbed her by her hair and brought his other hand to her throat. It looked like the lovely Miss Everleigh was in mighty hot water for sure, when—

"JOE MCGREW!" a powerful baritone rang out across the now-deserted town square. Bobcat Joe looked up in shock as The Stranger spun round in dramatic slow motion to face him. And with that, the dastardly varmint threw down Miss Everleigh like a sack o' seed corn and turned to his cold-faced accuser.

"Why, if it ain't my old pal Keanu," Bobcat sneered as he stalked the dusty streets toward The Stranger. "I'm surprised you've got the nerve to show your face round here, boy!"

"I've known devils in my day, Bobcat, but you're one of the worst. You have rained pain and suffering upon these people enough," muttered The Stranger in a voice so low you had to strain your ears to hear it. It sent a shiver down the spine of every man in town all the same. "You will leave this place and these good folks now, and you will do it quickly."

"And if'n I don't?" snarled Bobcat Joe, his finger stroking the trigger of the pistol he now had pointed squarely at The Stranger's chest.

"Then you reckon with me," said The Stranger. Bobcat threw back his head and laughed. "Boy, y'all just some Hollywood actor! You ain't a real tough guy! What makes you think y'all can mess with the most feared, vaguely anachronistic biker gang in Southern California?"

The Stranger smiled an enigmatic smile.

"Well, thanks to an upcoming movie I've already had extensive training for," said The Stranger, "I know kung fu." And with that he sent Bobcat Joe's pistol flying with the most graceful butterfly kick you ever did see. Before Joe could react, he was on his back, one scuffed taped-together shoe on his chest.

"I said, *leave*," growled The Stranger. Bobcat Joe was a-tremblin' now, and he looked around as wild-eyed as a cornered skunk for his fellow gang members.

"Stinky Jack?! Knuckles?! *Dave?!*"

The Stranger shook his head. "They're all gone."

"W-what did you do to them?!" wailed Bobcat Joe.

"I reunited Stinky Jack with his estranged daughter. I also paid for family therapy. I think he realizes how lucky he is to be given a second chance, so he's moved upstate to be closer to her. As for Knuckles . . . well, as you know, he suffered a rough childhood. We had a heart-to-heart about how just because he was written off by the world as a kid, doesn't mean he has to agree with the world, you know?"

Bobcat could only gasp, staring in silent horror at the man who had gotten him so licked but had hardly broken a sweat.

"It turns out that he always wanted to be a chef but didn't have the self-confidence to take it up professionally. I put him in touch with one of my buddies at an L.A. restaurant, and he's going to be living in my pool house while he gets his life together."

"And Dave?" whispered Bobcat Joe.

"Ah, Dave . . . ," said The Stranger. "I tried explaining to him how it's important to be vulnerable, and that as guys we are given a lot of messed up ideas about who we are and who we are meant to, like, *be*. I told him that he doesn't need to be the most violent dude out there to prove that he's a man. Like, he's already man enough! Then he tried to shoot me, so I killed him with a pencil."

Bobcat Joe cringed, for he knew that he'd been beat, and he knew that The Stranger knew it, too. "What are you going to do to me?" he whimpered. The Stranger cocked his head and stared at Bobcat just long enough to make him nervous, then released him. You didn't have to ask Bobcat Joe twice—he took the opportunity to skedaddle as fast as if he were pursued by the demons in *Constantine*.

No one knows where Bobcat Joe went after that day, but he was never seen in Damnation again. And as for The Stranger? Well, he stayed in town about a month or so, just so's folks could get themselves back on their feet again.

And because Governor Wilson had placed some mighty fearful budget cuts upon the California public school system, The Stranger brought in the finest of architects to design a new schoolhouse that was up to code, current with modern educational theory, and had at least ten rooms. He also hired a hundred men to build the place, and he stayed behind to help out with his own bare hands. Some say that in that time The Stranger accomplished the equivalent of a hundred men's work, but that's just a rumor.

Still, the time came that Miss Everleigh, the other

teachers, the children, and a hundred men were all dreading. The day the school was finished, it was time for The Stranger to take his leave. The Wachowskis were counting on him.

"I wish you could stay," Miss Everleigh told him true.

"I'm sorry, ma'am," The Stranger told her with a chaste kiss upon her hand and a heartfelt gaze. "But where I'm going, I must go alone. You see, I'm The One."

"I don't understand!" she gasped. He brought one work-roughened hand to her cheek.

"Not now. But you will." He smiled that devil-may-care yet definitely-caring mysterious smile of his. "You'd be surprised how literally I know that fact."

And with that, he got on his bike to ride away. All that he left behind in Damnation, California, were fond memories, good deeds, and a last call over his shoulder.

"Hey dudes," he laughed into the wind. "It might be time to rename the place."

"Keanu, come back!" sobbed the children. But if he heard, he didn't let on none, though a single tear fell down his cheek as he rode into the sunset.

Neither Miss Everleigh, nor the other folks, nor the kids, nor the hundred men ever saw him again. Some say he went on to film one of the greatest action movies of all time . . . twice. Some say he still rides the highway from time to time, perhaps to save still more poor souls in need.

But that's all just hearsay for another day, and another story.

PART V

Good and Evil and Keanu Reeves

Keanu Reeves is tricky. He's just as believable playing a hometown guy down on his luck as he is the chosen one who will save the human race from A) The Machines B) Demons C) Itself.

Keanu is able to play the everyman, the chosen man, and a mess of men in

between because he plays each one with emotional honesty and specificity, ramping up his intensity to match the scale of the movie.

If he were a character in a YA novel filled with capital-S Superpowers, his might be Cipher. Stand-In. Proxy. He creates a liminal space between the world of the story and our own, a portal we can pass through easily to access higher truths and good-ass times. We might not have the beauty or brawn or cutting sharp tongue of some of our favorite movie stars, but with Keanu Reeves, with *this* movie star, we always get to play with what's up his sleeve. Or, in some of the more dramatic entries in his catalogue, map our trauma onto his.

With his ability to contain and portray multitudes, along with his own eclectic choice in roles, we don't always know where Keanu's going to pop up in the cinematic landscape. He could show up to battle evil on a massive scale (*Constantine*) or wrestle evil quietly (with a couple kidney-punches) in some overgrown backyard of the soul. He could even appear as the embodiment of evil itself, cursing out Cate Blanchett for telling his beaten wife to leave him, wearing black leather pants (*The Gift*), or shivving an underground fighter to death for having the audacity to lose (*Man of Tai Chi*).

No matter where his characters fall on the spectrum of good and evil, his specificity and stoicism act as a grounding force in the stories he tells, no matter how tall the tale.

Keanu is KISS: a knight in story's service. Could his versatility be part of the same deal with the Devil he made to stay foxy forever?

KEANU: Good day, Devil. I would like to be able to play a wide variety of roles across generations and genres, all with a measure of believability and panache!

DEVIL: Yeah, yeah, cool, cool.

KEANU: . . . and look good doing it.

DEVIL: You got it, babe.

KEANU: Oh, and maybe I can win an Oscar, too? Or maybe a—

DEVIL: Catch ya later, dude! *Replicas* is gonna be great!

Taking the Good with the Baddies

We subscribe to the school of thought that movies can sometimes show us the best in ourselves, even while primarily serving as "escapist" entertainment. Movie stars are mythical avatars who help us understand who we are, who we should be, or who we could try to be—if we're up for it. But what good is recognizing the best in ourselves if we don't also take at least a sideways glance at the worst?

The Hero's Journey . . . to Hell!

One quality that makes Keanu a vivacious and versatile performer is his ability to play the hero with a thousand faces. Yes, maybe nine hundred of them are good guys: the as-good-as-or-slightly-better versions of ourselves we wish we could be, or maybe *really* could be on our very best days. Of those Goodies, you have a couple hundred Chosen Ones to work with—the *really* good guys. Maybe fifty are the worse-off-than-us guys who can't quite successfully break out of the escort-driving service or rob that bank after all.

But at least fifty more are the sinister faces of ourselves, the parts we suppress in muted agony. Ain't none of us good all the time—or maybe even bad all of the time. We're everything between those two poles. We all do our level best to walk in the path of the light.

But there are things sparkling in the dark.

Shiny things. Interesting things. Powerful things. We

try not to become mesmerized by them, but hey—maybe some of them are worth picking up, if only to cast them out again. Maybe some of them wouldn't be too bad to hold on to for a while, or a lifetime. Maybe some would rot our guts and corrupt our immortal souls. Whatever the temptation, and whatever succumbing to that temptation could mean for us and/or the good of all humankind, there's only so much tensile strength to our hearts to keep us from crossing over to the dark side. Some of Keanu's most interesting performances send us tumbling into that deep, delicious dark side before snatching us back to safety.

The Dark Side of the 'Nu

Keanu has a steady relationship with Good and an open relationship with Evil. Like pleather, it can be complicated.

He will fight evil, he will be evil, he will let evil try to tempt him into creating an incestuous devil baby to rule the mortal earth. There's something about watching someone we identify with cross over to the dark side—or even wrestle with the dark side's literal and figurative minions—that can feel so safe, yet adventurous and thrilling. If you've ever felt drunk with power trying on all the nail polish testers at the makeup store, you know the feeling.

Let us now slide into Keanu's DMs (Dangerous Men) and have a gander at the darkness on the edge of his town . . . and ours.

Constantine (2005)

Constantine is a kaleidoscopic stained-glass showcase for both "Keanu Reeves: Every Guy" and "Keanu Reeves: Chosen Guy." It's also a movie people get sassy about because it's not a faithful adaptation of the comic. (He isn't blond! Or English!) To that we say: there will be TV adaptations and *Supernatural* riffs to soothe your pain. In this singular entry in the theo-illogical, neo-noir oeuvre, Keanu plays with the full range of the good and gray and gross in all of us. He's like us regular folks (self-medicating, surly, one nice jacket to our name) as well as "blessed" with gifts from worlds beyond: he can press his forearms together and whisper Latin phrases to dispel evil, wield powerful and obscure theological weaponry, travel between dimensions using a bucket of water as a portal, and attract Rachel Weisz and Gavin Rossdale by turns.

Keanu anchors this story of a hell-bent man in a heaven-rent Los Angeles to the noir world, rooting the fantastic in the recognizable: he's a broken, self-centered detective who's seen it all—twice. The twist is, he'll never stop seeing it. Not even if he dies, because Constantine lives a life knowing his eternal soul will dwell in hell, thanks to a hard-luck technicality, which includes the ability to see *actual* demons from hell on the city bus.

Early in life, his character is cast off as an unbelievable loony tune by his family, and for that he suffers the ultimate price. When we meet him, he is (in Keanu's words) "hard-edged, hard-boiled, world-weary, cynical, fatalistic, nihilistic and self-interested, with a heart that may not be golden." He also wears a skinny tie!

In this, Keanu isn't playing *evil* but, rather, someone caught between good and bad. Some of the moments and choices that make his performance memorable are the tiny tendernesses tucked into a movie that strikes notes as big and bold as stained glass. He isn't just playing these moments to be a sweetheart or an asshole but to make Constantine a three-dimensional human being.

Keanu's physicality is called into broken-dream-ballet service here. His movements are sick and wet and lush, like the head of a lily hanging too heavy on its stem, swooping and bowing with uncanny grace. Then he shatters his own beauty with a crass line tossed off between cigarettes.

Not like anyone we really know, right?

The moments Keanu creates with his scene partners add a visceral depth to his otherwise stock noir hero. Serving as enemy (or irritant), Gavin Rossdale's half-demon character Balthazar dresses Constantine down in such close proximity (which Keanu receives with raised eyebrows but no flinching) that the two emanate a wicked and divine closeness that remains otherwise unspoken in the film. We get a heavy dose of history from a look that lasts mere moments before we drop it and move on. Such is life. Similarly, Constantine's interactions with Djimon Hounsou's Papa Midnite crackle with daring intimacy. But the relationship the movie serves is between Constantine and the troubled cop he must work with to solve a heart-wrenching mystery. Rachel Weisz, as the clearly not-meaningfully named Angela Dodson, has more than a little to do with Constantine's attempts to strive and thrive, even in the face of damnation.

The characters play to each other more as equals than typical love interests, but the small moments Keanu creates in his performance speak more to romance than good-versus-evil showdown cinema. He must show Angela hell—and with a quickness. The only way to do so is to sort of drown her. He takes charge, even though she's no wilting flower, and cradles her head as she enters the portal-bath he draws. Moments later, he holds her head underwater as she thrashes for long, terrible seconds. Anything to get you to hell so you can learn how your twin sister really died, babe.

In anticipation of this deep dive, he holds out his hands, waiting to receive her personal effects before plunging her gently into a demon-infested nightmare. No one needs a wet purse when they're conducting an investigation into the deepest depths of personal horror!

Also to note (and to blame on the early aughts): within this bathtub scene is a groan-worthy yet on-point noir "joke" in which Angela wonders if she needs to remove all her clothes to properly transition. Keanu is not *quite* smarmy enough to play this lightly when he responds with, "I'm thinking . . . no." We all politely occupy ourselves by looking at the bath tile of our choice as said joke falls flat and rolls out of view; one might even silently applaud Keanu for visually disengaging from this unsuccessful bit of "comedy."

Other intimacies created outside that unholy bathroom include Keanu providing an irritated, if protective, attitude toward his assistant, who is prone to repeating the name John every two seconds (bless you, Shia LaBeouf), and a scene in which Keanu and Rachel share a meal at an impeccably lit diner. Over their luminous fries and pancakes, their haunted faces glow with respect and interest for each other. Keanu also clasps a charmed amulet to her neck in an SUV, pre-heaven-and-hell showdown. Not only is it swoonworthy how close their beautiful heads are, but the man actually knows how to clasp a necklace. He traps spiders with a wry sense of doom, he cracks wise, he is nice to cats, and he likes that one noodle place over there behind the demon infestation.

Keanu doesn't hang a lantern on these little hooks of humanity. They simply provide color and life in a movie about war on an outsize stage. That's what the big battles are fought for, ultimately: the little lives. He plays everything with a light touch, which makes Constantine feel real, and the exaggerated world of the movie along with him. He tethers us to him, and together we drop into the depths of hell or float up to the heights of heaven.

Constantine is broken and ornery, but he has a grudging concern for the world around him. Keanu's portrayal shows us we can still give a shit while we're in the shit—even if, like Constantine, we're in the shittiest shit there is.

The devil is in the details, y'all.

DARKNESS LEVEL: Stars: They're Just Like Us!

The Devil's Advocate (1997)

Oh whoa, whoa, whoa, you're saying. *Keanu's Kevin Lomax isn't the bad guy in this movie! The bad guy is the literal devil, Al Pacino! In fact, Keanu gets one over on the Devil and de facto saves the world!* Sure, we say. But that's only in the final five minutes of the film's 2:38 runtime, after he spends the bulk of the movie selling out his wife, played by Charlize Theron, bit by bit. He doesn't even work that hard within the evil law firm but merely kisses ass because he knows it'd be a great career opportunity. The movie opens with a scene that shows Keanu as a no-lose lawyer: one with some disgust for his wretched clients, even if he knows he's good enough (or lucky and shameless enough) to get them off. Yet he also clearly loves his wife, even affectionately nibbling her pencil-skirt-sheathed rear end at a dive bar in celebration of his stomach-churning streak getting a guilty-as-hell child molester off scot-free.

But when Kevin is plucked from grand Floridian obscurity for a plum role at an elite firm in New York, Keanu shows us a man losing track of what should matter in life in favor of the spoils of success. As his normally bold and brassy wife's insecurities take root and her suspicions take hold, Kevin is all but absent during her subsequent breakdowns. When he *is* around, he's distracted by thoughts of his own glory (and a red-headed babe at the office). He's given multiple opportunities to believe the woman he's pledged his life to but confesses to the Devil himself that he'll resent her for throwing him off track, even if it's for a good reason.

Keanu plays Kevin as haunted and haughty in equal measure. Even if his accent isn't always consistent, his descent into douchiness via his ascent into his wildest dreams is right on the money.

DARKNESS LEVEL: Most heterosexual relationships you know.

Knock Knock (2015)

Keanu plays your run-of-the-mill, decent-seeming, handsome family man with a beautiful home and some sort of successful architect job. But when two hot young thangs show up at his house one rainy night when his wife and kid are out town, he lets them in—and his indulgences get the better of him. The girls repay him the only way they know how: with torture, ruin by social media, and threat of death! His character delivers what Keanu has called "an aria of self-defense," blaming the women for his misdeeds "when really it was his fault and his decision."

DARKNESS LEVEL: Opinionated chump on social media schooled hard by one of your mutual friends.

John Wick (2014)

Do we root for John Wick, reluctant but perfect assassin, even as he kills too many people for anyone other than podcast hosts to count, at least three of them with a pencil?

Yes.

Do we cheer and sparkle with the sheer joy of life as he rains retribution down on the bad guys because we *know* he's fighting to reclaim his life and is only killing *really* bad guys, which the movie takes abundant pains to point out? Do we continue to root for him because his is a life steeped in grief and a trap he can never escape because his problems are of his own making and the further he goes into the depths of hell, the further his dreams of life aboveground turn to dust in the wind? Do we enjoy spending time in John Wick's world, in which there are clear consequences for breaking the rules—because at least in John Wick's world there is a sense things are supposed to make—whereas in our world, everything contains more shades of gray than one of John's suits? Do we wish for a space like the Continental, where we can feel safe (at least in the first movie) and just have a damn drink?

Yes, yes, yes, and yes.

Do we love this movie because also . . . the clothes are great? Hell yes.

DARKNESS LEVEL: Blood that won't ever wash out.

The Bad Batch (2017)

The Bad Batch is an aggressively atmospheric, sour-gummy-candy-colored hellscape of a film. Keanu plays "The Dream," a gently aging DJ in a *Mad Max*–esque dystopia, where DJs are somehow still of use. Keanu's character is out to build himself a harem of honeys and graciously lets his subjects eat instant soup while he does so. To be fair, it seems that the alternative to Cuppa Noodle in this reality is cannibalism.

Keanu uses his at-hand "surfer vibes" to coolly conscript babes into his sex-slave service in exchange for better food than dehydrated pasta. The world is ugly and hard, he is soft and sweet, so really, what harm could it do to help yourself?

Keanu strikes a subdued note as a shrugging bad guy. Also of note, his physicality is a bit softer than in most films. A handsome schlub using his looks, his beats, and his chill attitude to make a killing in the land of the living dead. DARKNESS LEVEL: Softboy.

The Gift (2000)

Donnie Barksdale is scary. A tough customer who hates witches and fidelity, Keanu's take on a Southern stereotype is rich with familiarity and horror. Just barely restraining his inner rage at all times, he's capable of an emotional break whenever the mood strikes just right. Whether he's cupping a child's cheek in a display of dominance, using the most threadbare veneer of "politeness" to force his will on Cate Blanchett, or out-and-out physically abusing his wife and/or mistress, Keanu's Donnie knows how to position himself to get his way. Even if everyone else in town correctly estimates him as some dummy with a truck, he knows he's willing to cross whatever line necessary to protect himself—and keep the women around him in line.

DARKNESS LEVEL: That guy who freaks you out at the bar. And the school event. And the church social.

Bill & Ted's Bogus Journey (1991)

Evil Ted is very not excellent. And he wants you dead, dude!
DARKNESS LEVEL: Yourself on your worst day.

Much Ado About Nothing (1993)

Don John is too to be inconvenienced by petty contrivances like consent and the happiness of others. Selfish and petulant and impossible, Keanu's Don John is a study in selfishness by way of righteous jealousy. He's out to ruin everyone's fun because he thinks that, without doing so, he can never have his own. Shameful, especially considering if he got a good look at himself while he was being oiled by lesser-thans. He could have just had faith that something good was bound to happen, sooner or later.

Also, isn't it wicked that Keanu Reeves was this handsome when a good majority of his current superfans were in third grade?
DARKNESS LEVEL: Black leather pants on a summer's day.

The Watcher (2000)

Keanu plays a straight-up serial killer in this Chicago-set thriller that he was legally strong-armed into starring in.

His hair might be floppy, but his heart is hard and ice cold as he stalks women and offs them with some piano wire and a little soft-shoe. He cares less about the girls and more about the long-suffering cop who is always a step behind him—James Spader!

DARKNESS LEVEL: Burnt toast . . . that could kill you.

Man of Tai Chi (2013)

Keanu's Donaka Mark suffers no fools—and no losers. He knows what he wants with clear-cut passion, precision, and deadly accuracy: winners. He also falls prey to the ultimate seduction: corrupting a good soul. While he stokes the flames within the innocent-seeming tai chi whiz kid Tiger Chen—feeding the man's desires with glory and power—he never seems to think he'll get burned. LOL, Evil Keanu. LOL, we say.

DARKNESS LEVEL: "You owe me a life." Well, you never said *whose*.

Keanu has played more bad guys than this, and he'll likely play more still. There is a relish he lends his villainous characters, and a conflicted, hidden hope with which he graces those characters straddling the edge of good and evil.

Keanu has said that villains know what they want. Heroes are searching for the good, constantly wondering, always evaluating what they might find. Good guys lag behind because they spend so much time trying to weigh right and wrong. Bad guys strike quickly because they know what they want and what they're willing to give up to attain it.

Just some food for thought the next time you're snacking at a noodle cart before your next big battle between the forces of good and evil.

JOHNNY MEME-ONIC

Keanu Reeves. He may be a Man. He may be a Legend. But in a weird quirk of modern celebrity, he is also famously a Meme.

Yes, other celebrities have had their moments of internet glory. Maybe it's an awkward publicity shot that everyone feels they must react to on Twitter. Perhaps it's their one big reaction gif—the one we can instantly picture just by the description. (Vehemently clapping Dwayne "The Rock" Johnson! Meryl Streep pointing! Chris Tucker and Ice Cube's collective horror in *Friday*!) Heck, if the celebrity is male, handsome, and very lucky, he might even get to become the Internet's Boyfriend for a few glorious months before being tossed aside for one of the Chrises.

But none, *none*, have managed such dominance, such repeat success, such *longevity* as our man from Canada. The internet loves Keanu, often in a way more reminiscent of a creepy *SVU* suspect with a shrine in his basement. Here, we shall examine why.

Why So Sad?

On June 3, 2010, Reddit user rockon4life changed internet history.

Titled "Keanu. More sadness in comments" and posted to the much-visited r/pics subreddit, it was at first glance a deceptively simple series of tabloid shots of one Keanu Charles Reeves, sitting by himself with a sandwich on a park bench. His hair and beard are disheveled, his dad trainers clash with his smart blazer, and he consumes his lunch with all the practiced tragedy of a character in a '60s French arthouse movie. Small red text over the images bears the legend:

> I really enjoy acting.
> Because when I act, I'm no longer me.

And that, in the way it sometimes goes with these things, was that.

Soon the Sad Keanu memes were coming in thick and fast. The following day on Reddit, multiple threads expanded on Keanu's ennui, and up popped Photoshopped images of the many places Keanu could be sad. Sad Keanu rode an eagle and ate lunch atop a skyscraper. He joined Barack Obama in the Situation Room and turned out to be the person Forrest Gump was talking to all along. Just a few days later, it reached the saturation point, with confused Redditors posting threads begging someone to explain exactly "why this sudden obsession with Keanu Reeves?"

But Sad Keanu was bigger than Reddit. It was only a matter of time before our hero's legend spread; he soon conquered Twitter, Facebook, and Tumblr with his bread-and-meat-flavored sorrow. Within five days, the meme had its own Buzzfeed listicle. By June 14, the single-topic website SadKeanu.com had launched, collecting all the memes in one easy-access source.

Sad Keanu mania reached its zenith on June 15, with Cheer Up Keanu Day. Publicized with fan-made videos and graphics, participants were encouraged to send love letters, phone calls, charity donations, or gifts of any kind—a showing of mass kindness in an attempt to make the actor crack a smile. It was an early example of the collective power of the internet to gather large amounts of strangers to do something ridiculous, this time for good.

It couldn't last, of course. On June 17, SadKeanu.com received a DMCA takedown notice by the owner of the images, and gradually, slowly, the flood of Mr. Reeves looking mopey began to recede from the internet's collective attention. At this point, everyone should have recovered the way they normally do after a burst of directed irony: find a new celebrity to stan.

They did not.

"Cometh the hour, cometh the meme"

People today forget how novel it once was to be able to talk back to the media you consumed, but as recently as the mid-2000s, internet content was generally produced according to a traditional publishing model. In this model, clever (or well-connected) people worked their way up to become Arbiters of Thought and Taste. Once these individuals had scaled that sacred citadel, they would receive an opportunity the rest of us could only dream of: the chance to spread their opinions across the world to a waiting audience.

Social media screwed all that up. Where once every piece of media had to be funneled through a series of gatekeepers before distribution to the public, now a whole new world opened up. A weird world in which ordinary folk could make a lasting impact on popular culture, like a graffiti tag across a billboard. Their thoughts, their words, their personal interests were broadcast far and wide for all to see and ponder, just like those of the Official Tastemakers.

And like a long-lost love the public had finally reunited with, they were Never Letting Keanu Go. Torn asunder from Sad Keanu by the law, a new Keanu meme was waiting in the wings to comfort the internet in its time of loss.

It began, in the way of many internet things, extremely randomly. To be specific, slide 22 of "*Vulture*'s Complete Field Guide to the Facial Expressions of Keanu Reeves." Published on December 11, 2008, in *New York* magazine's *Vulture* blog, the slide shows a still from *Bill & Ted's Excellent Adventure* that features a very young, mushroom-haired Keanu as he stares into the middle distance, displaying a look that is simultaneously terrified and confused. The caption reads:

Emotion: Fear
Year depicted: 1989
Habitat: Bill & Ted's Excellent Adventure
Field notes: A group of medieval knights are
seconds away from killing Keanu.

Looking at it, you could almost hear the "whoa." And perhaps for that reason it started cropping up as a reaction in various online forums, but only on rare occasions.

Not until the meme mutated into an early Advice Animals image macro series (the popular layout composed of white Impact text over a photo) did the whole thing really take off. The first meme of its kind to feature this image was posted on the r/funny subreddit on June 2, 2011. In it, Keanu's horror is no longer due to imminent death by mace but to Deep Conspiracy Thoughts floating above and below his stricken face.

What if we CAN breathe in space
and they just don't want us to escape

The distinctive Advice Animals Impact font was not yet deployed here, but Conspiracy Keanu had been born. And just like a beautiful newborn foal, the meme was initially a little shaky. Save just one other post (entitled "WHAT IF ALL THE SPECS WE SEE IN THE LIGHT / ARE ALL JUST MINIATURE UNIVERSES?"), submitted to the humor site FunnyJunk on September 24, 2011, and notable only for the first use of the Advice Animals format, nothing new appeared until November 2011.

Yet once the internet learned of this new Keanu meme, its assured rise was meteoric. The meme was in full swing within a few days, with images appearing at a rate of digital knots. Conspiracy Keanu's doubting and troubled face floated eternally over such musings as:

WHAT IF THE CIA INVENTED DINOSAURS
TO DISCOURAGE TIME TRAVEL?

WHAT IF CATS HAVE THEIR OWN INTERNET
AND IT'S FULL OF PICTURES OF US?

WHAT IF KEANU REEVES CREATED THIS MEME
TO BECOME AN INTERNET CELEBRITY AGAIN?

Next was the launch of a Facebook fan page on November 19. Not long after, listicles of the best images were posted to various sites, including BuzzFeed and UPROXX, the same day they appeared. The domain for the single-topic blog ConspiracyKeanu.com was registered on December 18. By April 2012, the Quickmeme page had an astonishing 37,458 submissions, all for Conspiracy Keanu.

But the internet's thirst for Keanu memes could not be slaked. A series of photos of him doing tai chi were inevitably jumped on and transformed into dramatic action series or mundane pizza-delivery sequences. Sad Keanu reappeared in the edgy spinoff Sad Keanu in a Helmet. The saga finally came full circle with the emergence of Happy Keanu: a still of him gamboling through the streets, camera in hand, from the film *Generation Um.*

The news that Sad Keanu was now Happy Keanu was so big that even the *Washington Post* covered it. On January 18, 2011, the BBC questioned the man himself about his thoughts on his memehood. True to form, he described it as "good clean fun." Sad Keanu was now Serious News.

Righteous

So far, so ironic—and so 2000s. Keanu's 2010 reemergence, from slightly out-of-date 1990s has-been to King of the Internet, was a perfect encapsulation of the twin sides of popular culture during the terrible time that was the Great Recession: the encroaching darkness and the ironic laughter in the face of the gloom. A relic of a more innocent era, when people were aware of how screwed up things were but still believed that if we just made fun of everything hard enough, sanity would somehow restore itself. A time when folks thought of themselves as cynics but were, in hindsight, as hopelessly naive as any well-intentioned adult advising kids to "just laugh at and ignore the bullies."

Maybe. But a quick click on the link to that very first Sad Keanu meme shows hints of something more, nestled within the comments. Something that would come to dominate how we see Keanu and punctuate his rebirth from adorable joke to God Amongst Men and, with it, a reassessment of what we value in male behavior. It's not just an accurate identification of the disease, it's a potential cure.

Back to the thread. It all started when user u/bo2dd2 left a comment, sharing a sweet anecdote about his experiences as assistant prop designer on the set of *Chain Reaction*. This post alone gained over two thousand upvotes:

> EVERY DAY for the last few weeks of filming, Keanu treated the stage hands and "grunt workers" (including myself) by taking us out for free breakfast and lunch. He was genuinely a very nice guy to work with. Since then, I've worked on about 30 different sets and have never met an actor as generous and friendly as him.

In the past, this might have remained a cool personal story, albeit one brought up regularly at parties. Now, however, things had changed. Run-ins with someone famous could be shared with the world. A new phenomenon appeared: inside knowledge collated from hundreds of ordinary folk who claimed to have had an encounter with a star, viewed and shared across social media for all to see. And with that, celebrities gained a reputation for niceness or nastiness that couldn't be controlled by even the most ferocious publicist.

And so it goes. The comments in this particular thread quickly turned into a collection of various Redditors' personal Keanu stories. The tone of these comments has the breathlessness of teenagers talking about Regina George at the beginning of *Mean Girls*, but the tales they tell describe a modern-day saint who would do anything to help his fellow man.

On and on they flow, each more lovely than the last. Keanu gave a poor set builder a $20,000 Christmas bonus to help his family out! And when a Redditor's friend was stranded on the highway, Keanu pulled over, tried to jump-start her car, then called AAA and drove fifty miles out of his way to drop her off!! Keanu bought all of the special effects guys on *The Matrix Reloaded* Harleys for Christmas!!! Keanu is *the most sincere, humble and lovely dude he'd ever met* as well as *the bravest man he's ever met*!!!!

User u/greedyiguana summed it up: *are these stories all true? It's starting to sound like chuck norris jokes.*

They were on to something there, for Chuck Norris was indeed the internet's nostalgic celebrity meme machine before Keanu. Starting in 2005 and full of chest-thumping ironic bravado, the Chuck Norris Facts meme boasted things like:

Chuck Norris does not sleep. He waits.
Chuck Norris' tears cure cancer. Too bad he has never cried.
Fire escapes were invented to protect fire from Chuck Norris.
Chuck Norris once visited the Virgin Islands. They are now The Islands.

> Once a cobra bit Chuck Norris' leg. After five
> days of excruciating pain, the cobra died.
> Chuck Norris died ten years ago, but the Grim
> Reaper can't get up the courage to tell him.
> Leading hand sanitizers claim they can kill 99.9
> percent of germs; Chuck Norris can kill 100
> percent of whatever the fuck he wants

These hyperbolic factoids were ostensibly ironic . . . but only to a point. For within this characterization of the actor and martial artist as the ultimate in toughness, virility, and sheer alpha-maleness was a celebration of a certain type of masculine archetype, one that also fed into existing beliefs about what a man should aspire to be, spread across a thousand ads and Zack Snyder movies of that era. Chuck Norris was the Manliest of Men in a highly specific way: he did what he wanted, fucked who he wanted, relied on no one, and no one dared defy him. Chuck Norris's awesomeness was part of the joke, not a sarcastic comment on what he lacked.

In short, it couldn't be more different from the sad and questioning figure of the Keanu memes. That toughness might have flown in the America! Fuck Yeah! years of the War on Terror, but by 2010 we were broke, exhausted, and had less patience for the macho-man types who'd gotten us into this mess. We were crying out, parched for another sort of hero. One who was gentle. One who was kind. One who, at the very least, didn't act like a total dickhead.

In the early days of Sad Keanu's rise, this shift was called out directly on Reddit with the thread "Instead of Chuck Norris, let's make Keanu Reeves a meme" and further elaborated by its poster: "Just sayin, guy's awesome." Likewise, on that first Sad Keanu thread, user u/TARDIS summed it up:

> Look at him, on that bench, eating a sandwich like anyone else. He's human. He's not some damned robot or your typical tool of the media. He's just another guy trying to do his thing and live his life . . . that's pretty damned magical, if you ask me. so, I don't know why everyone ELSE is "obsessed" with him or supports him, but I do it because he's a great human being, and frankly, one hell of an actor.

It was Keanu as ordinary man, not movie star, trying to be good and do his best in the wake of personal tragedy, that resonated in the public's imagination. A normality and a vulnerability, combined with goodness, even in the face of everything being messed up beyond all recognition. It is these qualities that separate him in the internet's imagination from the rest of the nostalgic childhood figures we occasionally bring up sarcastically to remind ourselves of better times.

The Story Continues

So what now, in these dark days of a post-Brexit, post-Trump world? Well, like many of us, meme-verse Keanu has adapted . . . and he is angry.

The shot that inspired the newest meme is, admittedly, awesome. Taken from the set of *John Wick 3* and rising to prominence in August 2018, it features our hero, on a horse, gun pointed at the cyclist chasing him, his expression a rictus of righteous fury. It was quickly dubbed Brutal Keanu, and wags on Twitter were quick to respond, including @arya_starke, who called him "the murder prince we deserve." The meme was even updated for the format of our times, with John Wick labeled me, the cyclist he is shooting urge to sleep, and the horse pug videos at 3 am. In short, the snark of the early days of Advice Animals is back, this time with a side order of self-deprecation and rage.

It's entirely unsurprising that in these troubled times we would turn to the figure of Keanu Reeves as he appears in *John Wick*. Vulnerable, yet terrifying. Hurt, and willing to dole out the same to those who hurt him. Sad, but with a grim determination of what needs to be done. Yes, once again, the public has projected the spirit of the age upon Keanu's enigmatic face.

At time of press, a new Keanu meme has come on the scene: You're Breathtaking Keanu. It's based on Keanu's uplifting response to the world's most wholesome heckler during his presentation at the E3 conference. Someone yelled "You're breathtaking!" and Keanu responded with "You're breathtaking! You're all breathtaking!" Breathtaking Keanu has been taking the internet by storm of late, making us all feel a bit better about things.

It is perhaps this capacity to be both Everyman and

Superman that accounts for the strange longevity of both "Keanu as meme" and "Keanu as star." It's his ability to transform into the perfect archetype onto which we can project our hopes and emotions, both on the screen and in our imagination. What we have ached for, what we want to believe in, is simply the idea of Keanu as one of us, but better than us. A mythic figure of legend that we all aspire, in some way, to be.

Notes

Sources cited and consulted during our research

Bim Adewunmi and Nichole Perkins, "Keanu," November 22, 2017, season one, episode five of *Thirst Aid Kit*, a podcast produced by *BuzzFeed*, https://thirstaidkitpodcast.tumblr.com/episodes.

Angelica Jade Bastién, "The Grace of Keanu Reeves," *Bright Wall/ Dark Room*, Issue 32: The Unloved, February 2016, https://www .brightwalldarkroom.com/2016/04/21/the-grace-of-keanu-reeves/.

Sheila Benson, "'Record' Focuses on Aftershocks of Teen Suicides," review of *Permanent Record*, directed by Marisa Silver, *Los Angeles Times*, April 22, 1988.

James Cameron-Wilson, "Pseudo-Quasi-Method in His Madness," review of *Point Break*, directed by Kathryn Bigelow, *Film Review*, November 1991.

Vincent Canby, "A Road Movie about Male Hustlers," review of *My Own Private Idaho*, directed by Gus Van Sant, *New York Times*, September 27, 1991, https://www.nytimes.com/1991/09/27/movies/ reviews-film-festival-a-road-movie-about-male-hustlers.html.

Scott Collura, "Keanu Reeves Wants Revenge on the Set of John Wick," *IGN*, September 10, 2014, https://www.ign.com/ articles/2014/09/10/keanu-reeves-wants-revenge-on-the-set-of-john-wick.

Richard Corliss, "Caught Between Heaven and Hell," review of *Constantine*, directed by Francis Lawrence, *Time*, February 14, 2005.

Roger Ebert, review of *Bill and Ted's Bogus Journey*, *Chicago Sun-Times*, July 19, 1991.

Roger Ebert, review of *Speed*, *Chicago Sun-Times*, June 10, 1994.

Roger Ebert, "Keanu Thought His Two Years Were Running Out," *Chicago Sun-Times*, April 7, 1996.

Matt Edwards, "Chad Stahelski interview: *John Wick 2, Highlander*," *Den of Geek*, February 17, 2017, https://www.denofgeek.com/uk/movies/john-wick-chapter-2/47347/chad-stahelski-interview-john-wick-2-highlander.

Larry Fitzmaurice, "Nicolas Winding Refn on the Joys of Vinyl and the Transcendent Keanu Reeves," *Vulture*, June 5, 2015, https://www.vulture.com/2015/06/nicolas-winding-refn-on-keanu-and-crate-digging.html.

Owen Gleiberman, review of *Point Break*, directed by Kathryn Bigelow, *Entertainment Weekly*, July 26, 1991.

"Keanu Being Awesome" subreddit, https://www.reddit.com/r/KeanuBeingAwesome.

Know Your Meme, "Sad Keanu," https://knowyourmeme.com/memes/sad-keanu.

Tim Lammer, "Director Raimi Has 'The Gift'," review of *The Gift*, directed by Sam Raimi, *The Boston Channel*, January 12, 2001.

Patrick Lee, "Hell Bent," *Sci Fi Magazine*, February 2005.

Roger Lewis, "Most Excellent Prince," review of *Hamlet*, directed by Lewis Baumander, Manitoba Theatre Centre, the *Sunday Times*, January 22, 1995.

Rob Lowing, "Keanu's Excellent Career," *Sydney Morning Herald*, September 23,1993.

Leilani Nishime, *Undercover Asian: Multiracial Asian Americans in Visual Culture* (Chicago: University of Illinois Press, 2013).

Priscilla Page, "The World of JOHN WICK," review of *John Wick*, directed by Chad Stahelski and David Leitch, *Birth. Movies. Death.*, March 31, 2016 https://birthmoviesdeath.com/2016/03/31/the-world-of-john-wick

Christine Radish, "A Very Special Gift," *X-posé*, February 2001.

Peter Rainer, "Engaging Falk Provides Lift for a Wearying 'Tune in Tomorrow'," review of *Tune in Tomorrow*, directed by Jon Amiel, *Los Angeles Times*, November 2, 1990.

Carrie Rickey, "Keanu Reeves: Quiet Power," *Greensboro News & Record*, June 18, 1994.

Bonnie Steele, "Having a ball with Keanu Reeves," *Valley*, October 2000.

Bob Thompson, "Keanu as nasty as can be," *Toronto Sun*, January 14, 2001.

Fred Topel, "Pros and Constantine," review of *Constantine*, directed by Francis Lawrence, Entertainment Today, Februrary 11-17, 2005.

Whoa Is (Not) Me, https://www.whoaisnotme.net.

There is a tweet, somewhere out there, that posits that Keanu was vampirized on *Bram Stoker's Dracula*, but we can't find it. Wherever you are, fair tweeter, we are sorry we couldn't acknowledge you.

Acknowledgments

Kitty and Larissa would like to thank their friends and families for their endless love and support, and for being game for months of research. Some of you were elated while others groaned, but in the end we thank you all for letting Keanu into your hearts—and further embedding him into ours.

We would also like to thank the entire team at Quirk Books for bringing this book to life. It's a tricky task to make a book like this a reality, and this team broke the Matrix and then some to make it a reality that's far from anything The Machines could dream up. Thank you to Jhanteigh Kupihea for your excited phone calls and brilliant edits. Thank you to Ivy Weir, Christina Schillaci, Nicole De Jackmo, and the entire PR and marketing team for your innovation and dedication to getting the word out. Thank you to Aurora Parlagreco and Andie Reid on the design team for making this book as powerful and beautiful as Keanu himself. Thank you to Rebecca Gyllenhaal for her editorial assistance.

Endless thanks to Tres Dean, author of *For Your Consideration: Dwayne "The Rock" Johnson*, for being an energetic and warm collaborator in the beginning of FYC.

A most special thanks to Maure Luke, a master storyteller and Keanu scholar, for her wisdom, patience, and education. *The Replacements* and redemption for ever and ever.

Thank you, reader, for joining us on this most excellent adventure.

Finally, thank you to Keanu Reeves. You've made so much we love—and you've made a world of people happy.

About the Authors

Kitty Curran and Larissa Zageris are a creative duo based out of Chicago. *My Lady's Choosing*, their interactive romance novel, is on best-of lists ranging from *Harper's Bazaar*, *Buzzfeed*, and the New York Public Library. They are the cocreators of the viral illustrated novel *Taylor Swift: Girl Detective in The Secrets of the Starbucks Lovers*. Their most recent comic together, *13 Go Mad in Wiltshire*, appeared in *The Wicked + The Divine: The Funnies #1* from Image Comics. They have a TV pilot in the second round of the 2019 Sundance Episodic Lab. They think it is most righteous that their second book with Quirk Books is about someone they—and so many—love so dearly.

Larissa grew up in Midlothian, IL, and studied screen-writing and film at New York University. In addition to prose, she also writes for the stage and screen. She, like Mr. Reeves, is a power Virgo.

Kitty grew up in London, where she was but a mere baby stan of Mr. Reeves. She is now a grown-up Keanu stan who lives in Chicago and writes books, makes comics, and illustrates what are essentially dad jokes in visual form. She also drinks a lot of tea.

Look out for these other titles in
the *For Your Consideration* series

Dwayne "The Rock" Johnson
Available now wherever books are sold

The Chrises
Available in May 2020

Maya Rudolph
Available in Fall 2020